A2 in a Week

English

Zoë Keeling and
Cherie Rowe,
Abbey College, Birmingham
Series Editor: Kevin Byrne

Where to find the information you need

Essay Writing	3
Style Toolbox	8
Drama Toolbox	13
Drama Application	21
Drama Question Examination Toolbox	30
Prose Toolbox	36
Pre-1900 Prose Application	41
Post-1900 Prose Application	50
Poetry Toolbox	55
Poetry Application	60
Chaucer Toolbox and Application	66
Synoptic Paper	74
Exam Practice Questions	77
Use your Knowledge Answers	78

Letts Educational
4 Grosvenor Place, London SW1X 7DL
School enquiries: 01539 564910
Parent & student enquiries: 01539 564913
E-mail: mail@lettsed.co.uk

Website: www.letts-educational.com

First published 2001
10 9 8 7 6 5

British Library Cataloguing in Publication Data
A CIP record for this book is available from the British Library.

ISBN 978-1-84315-815-8

Cover design by Purple, London

Prepared by *specialist* publishing services, Milton Keynes

Printed in Dubai

Essay Writing

20 minutes

Test your knowledge

1 Name four different types of essay question.

2 Tick the correct statement:
(a) You should write about characters in a novel as if they are real people.
(b) You should write about characters in a novel as creations of the author.

3 Is the following statement true or false?
'When I write an essay on a selection of poetry, I only need to use one or two poems to answer the question.'

4 Fill in the missing word.
'When I write about drama, I should always remember that a play is not just words on a page, but an event to be seen on _____ .'

5 Complete this sentence.
'When I write an essay, I must examine the title carefully and make sure that I answer the _____ .'

6, 7, 8: Match the structural parts of an essay with what should be written in them.

6 Introduction   (a) a paragraph in which my comments are drawn together and the question is answered concisely

7 Middle section   (b) a paragraph in which I identify the key issues and the questions raised by the essay title and identify how I am going to structure answering them

8 Conclusion   (c) a series of logically linked points to present an argument which answers the essay question in sectioned paragraphs with supporting quotation from the text

Answers

1 direct, quotation, treatment, passage 2 (b) 3 false 4 stage 5 question
6 (b) 7 (c) 8 (a)

 If you got them all right, skip to page 6

3

Essay Writing

30 minutes

Improve your knowledge

In *AS English in a Week*, you learnt how to structure and plan an essay using the three-step process, which ensures that you do not wander off the subject or re-tell the plot.

Key points from AS in a Week

Essay Writing
pages 9–14

At A2 level, the essay questions will be more complex and you will have to think carefully about what is really being asked before you start to plan your answer.

1 Usually questions come in four different forms:

- direct questions that start with how, why or what

- quotation questions that suggest an idea for discussion by quoting a statement about the text, which is often followed by an invitation for you to agree or disagree (you may find that you agree with some parts and not others)

- questions that ask you to consider the treatment of one or two aspects of the text

- passage questions that detail an excerpt from the text and ask you to comment on it in some way.

never re-write an essay that you have written before in an exam

2 Questions about novels tend to focus on character, theme, style and the attitude of the author. You may be asked how a character changes through a novel, or about a particular aspect of a character or about how you feel towards a character. Questions on themes tend to focus on how they emerge and change. Questions on style focus on the author's management of the plot, structure and language. Always remember to write about novels with the author in mind. Characters only exist in the author's creation of them so make sure that you do not write about them as if they are real people.

3 Questions on poetry tend to focus on style, theme, imagery, narrative techniques and use of stanza form. Questions often ask you to comment on the effectiveness of the poetry. When answering questions on poetry, you should refer to at least six or seven poems, not just one or two.

Essay Writing

4 Questions on drama are similar to those used for the novel, but they also ask questions on the dramatic effectiveness of plays. This means that you must consider the play as an event on a stage and not just words on a page.

5 The main complaint examiners have about students' essay writing is that students fail to answer the question. Students do not look closely enough at the essay title to establish what it is really asking them. So, read the question three or four times to determine exactly what it is asking. Decide what kind of question it is and look for the key words that tell you what the examiner wants from you. Try to break the question down into parts – some questions do this for you in their title and hence automatically create an essay plan.

6 Examiners are looking to see that you can understand the issues raised by the question. In your introduction, you should write a paragraph in which you explain the problems of the essay as you understand them and outline for the examiner what you are going to argue about them.

be confident to produce independent thoughts, as long as they can be well argued and well supported by the text

7 In the middle section of your essay, make sure that you produce a coherent argument so that you move from one point to the next in a logical way. You must show that you know which parts of the text provide evidence as proof of the argument by choosing appropriate quotes. When you use literary terminology, make sure that you show how the devices have an effect on the reader and how the meaning of the literature changes with their presence. Try to show how particular words or phrases influence the meaning of the text.

8 In the final paragraph, you must draw your comments together to produce a conclusion that answers the question.

always re-read your essays to correct spelling, grammar and punctuation mistakes

Essay Writing

45 minutes

Use your knowledge

1 Look carefully at the following essay titles. Identify a type of question for each.

(a) 'Gatsby is the only moral character in the novel.' How far do you agree with this statement?

(b) How does Pip's character grow and change through the novel *Great Expectations*?

(c) Comment on the narratorial voice in the following extract:

Mr Standfast by John Buchan

> I had received a C.B. for the Erzerum business, so what with these and my Matabele and South African medals and the Legion of Honour, I had a chest like the High Priest's breastplate. I rejoined in January, and got a brigade on the eve of Arras. There we had a star turn, and took about as many prisoners as we put infantry over the top. After that we were hauled out for a month, and subsequently planted in a bad bit on the Scarpe with a hint that we would soon be used for a big push. Then suddenly I was ordered home to report to the War Office, and passed on by them to Bullivant and his merry men. So here I was sitting in a railway carriage in a grey tweed suit, with a neat new suit-case on the rack labelled C.B. The initials stood for Cornelius Brand, for that was my name now. And an old boy in the corner was asking me questions and wondering audibly why I wasn't fighting.

(d) Discuss the ways in which the author treats different symbols through the novel.

2 Which of these sentences about a character in a novel exhibits a better style of essay writing?

(a) 'Paul grows up to be a mean and selfish young man and rarely thinks about others.'

(b) 'The author develops Paul's character through the novel into a mean and selfish young man, who is rarely shown to think about the other characters in the novel.'

Essay Writing

3 Identify how the imagery of the following lines of poetry helps to make the description of the scene effective:

Belfast Confetti

Suddenly as the riot squad moved in, it was raining exclamation marks,
Nuts, bolts, nails, car-keys. A fount of broken type. And the explosion
Itself – an asterisk on the map. This hyphenated line, a burst of rapid fire …
I was trying to complete a sentence in my head, but it kept stuttering,
All the alleyways and side-streets blocked with stops and colons.

Ciara Carson

4 Name four features that you should play close attention to when writing about drama, that you do not need to consider in poetry or novels.

5 Look closely at the following essay title. Pick out the key words in the title and explain what you understand them to mean.

'The dominant influence on the plot and subplot of *Much Ado About Nothing* is hearsay.' How far do you agree?

6 Write a first sentence for an introduction to the essay title in Question 5.

7 Which of these quotes makes good supporting evidence for the following point?

'Many of Wilfred Owen's war poems refer to the destructive power of dawn and the deadliness of night.'

(a) 'Northward, incessantly, the flickering gunnery rumbles
Far off, like a dull rumour of some other war.'

(b) 'Sunlight seems a blood-smear; night comes blood-black;
Dawn breaks open like a wound that bleeds afresh.'

(c) 'For though the summer oozed into their veins
Like an injected drug for their bodies' pains'

8 Name four words or phrases that should characterise your writing of a conclusion.

Style Toolbox

20 minutes

Test your knowledge

1 Is the following statement true or false?

'I should never use the first person "I" in an essay.'

2 Which of these sentences adopts the best essay style to describe this character:
- (a) 'Leo is a naïve boy who finds himself in an environment in which he has little understanding of the class issues that surround his close friend, Marcus Maudsley.'
- (b) 'The author presents Leo as a naïve boy who is shown to enter into an environment in which he has little understanding of the class issues that surround his close friend, Marcus Maudsley.'

3 Tick the correct statement:

- (a) 'When I write about a text, I should consider the author's perspective on what happens in the plot.'

- (b) 'When I write about a text, I only need to consider that the plot simply tells the story of the work.'

4 Give three words (other than 'reveal') that you could use to describe how a setting can reveal a character.

5 Connect the correct verbs in the right-hand column with the phrases in the left-hand column.
- (a) The symbols in the novel _____ the meaning.
- (b) The sounds in the poem are _____ throughout the stanza.
- (c) The metre of the poem is _____ in the first stanza.

(i) hesitant

(ii) express

(iii) shrill

Answers

1 False – you can use 'I' to express your own ideas, although the majority of your points should be made in the third person. 2 (b) 3 (a) 4 any three of: mirror, echo, represent, reflect, emulate 5 (a) (ii) (b) (iii) (c) (i)

 If you got them all right, skip to page 12

30 minutes

Improve your knowledge

In the Style Toolbox chapter of *AS English in a Week*, you learnt that you need to choose your words carefully when you write essays and that you should use vocabulary that is not too colloquial or informal. At best, your essay should be a pleasure for your examiner to read – you have chosen vocabulary that expresses your ideas accurately, concisely and logically through sentences that flow together. At worst, your essay style can mar the meaning of your work – the examiner does not understand your argument and has to spend too much time correcting spelling, punctuation and grammar.

If you still have problems with punctuation and grammar, you should try to resolve them before your exams – *GCSE English in a Week* has some useful tips to help you. It really is unforgivable to spell the names of characters or writers incorrectly – learn them carefully.

Many students at A2 level have plenty of good ideas to express, but worry about how to express them. The points below should help you to express your ideas in a more fluent and literary way.

Key points from AS in a Week

Style   pages 15–19

avoid abbreviation such as 'don't' and 'can't'

1   When you are discussing a work, it is best to use the third person (he or she) when talking about the reader or audience, but when you are writing about your own thoughts and feelings it is acceptable to use the first person (I).

2   It is important that in your writing you recognise that characters in a novel are created by the author and don't exist in their own right. Therefore it is essential that you do not write about how the author 'describes' a scene as if it were real, but how the author arranges, shapes, presents, shows or moulds the characters and scenes.

write about texts in the present tense, not the past tense

3   Whenever you are asked to write about the themes of a book, you should remember to write about the author's perspective on what he or she has presented.

Style Toolbox

 The relationship between character and setting can be important in a text and therefore the words that you use to describe this relationship are important too. You can use words and phrases like:

- the setting reflects a character

- the setting represents an aspect of a character

- the setting echoes aspects of a character

- the setting reveals the nature of a character.

 You will need to describe how symbols play a part in a text. Words that you can use to help express the influence of symbols are:

- the symbol represents…

- the symbol suggests…

- the symbolism evokes…

- this symbol expresses… .

don't try to use long words that you don't understand (and can't spell!)

When you want to write about the sounds that are used in a text, but particularly in poetry, you can use words that you might normally use to describe how people speak:

- the words are gentle

- the words are whispering

- the words seem smooth

- the words sound piercing

- the words grate

- the words sound shrill.

Rhythm is another aspect of poetry that is often difficult to describe. Since rhythm is connected closely with music, you can use musical words to describe the rhythm in a text, e.g.:

- the rhythm is uneven

- the rhythm is awkward

- the rhythm is regular

- the rhythm is heavy.

You can also use the term 'metre' instead of rhythm:

- the metre is erratic

- the metre is deliberate

- the metre is hesitant.

clear communication is the key

30 minutes

Use your knowledge

Carefully read the following excerpt from a student's essay. Underline all the features in the essay that you feel are poor style and suggest suitable alternatives.

On a passage from F Scott Fitzgerald's *The Great Gatsby*

1 The text concerned showed the over-indulgence of a party, showing up the
2 shallowness and superficiality of the people there as they got progressively drunk.
3 Gatsby doesn't seem to be around, and in not being at his own debauched party,
4 I think shows he's truly 'great', like it says in the title of the novel.

5 The text was written in the first person and the author observed the party from
6 his house next door. He wasn't invited, probably because he's not interested in
7 going, but in describing the actions of the guests at the party, the author shows
8 that he thinks that they're not very nice people, since they drink a lot and can't
9 remember each other's names.

10 There were lots of literary devices used like similes and metaphors and they were
11 very effective. Scott Fitzroy used lots of colours in the description, which I think
12 made the scene look bright and cheerful.

Drama Toolbox

20 minutes

Test your knowledge

It is important that you understand:

- what the assessment objectives are
- where the assessment objectives apply to the study of your drama text
- how you can best revise and prepare to meet the assessment objectives in the examination.

The Drama Toolbox will test your knowledge about your assessment objectives and show you where they fit into your study of drama text. This chapter will also give you valuable examination advice as to how you can meet those assessment objectives

The Drama Application chapter will test your knowledge about applying those assessment objectives to an extract, give you examples and further help and then ask you to apply the assessment objectives to your own drama text.

1 Assessment Objective 1 (AO1) is how well you can use the appropriate terminology to describe literary effects and whether you can write an argument in a coherent and organised style.

2 Assessment Objective 2ii (AO2ii) looks at how well you can explore and make comparisons between literary texts. You should show that you understand how the play you are studying fits into its genre.

3 Assessment Objective 3 (AO3) is where an examiner will be assessing your ability to show detailed understanding of the ways in which the dramatist has chosen the form, structure and language to shape the meaning of the play.

4 Assessment Objective 4 (AO4) is where your show that you can analyse other viewpoints and be confident in putting forward your own opinion with clear textual evidence in response to a statement about the play you are studying.

5 Assessment Objective 5 (AO5) is where you show the examiner that you understand the cultural, historical and contextual influences on the text you are studying.

45 minutes

Improve your knowledge

1 The assessment objective for coherence, organisation and terminology tests your ability to produce a consistently logical argument. Each paragraph should be arranged methodically in order to convey your argument. The following is the kind of question you may be asked in the examination:

'Which do you consider to be the most powerful and dramatic tragedy in the play *King Lear*, Lear's death or Cordelia's death?'

Now study the student's essay plan below as an example of a logical and methodically structured argument.

Key points from AS in a Week

Drama
pages 20–27
pages 28–36
pages 46–53

always use literary terms in your essays to explain your understanding of the text

Question breakdown	King Lear	Cordelia
Tragedy	• Eponymous hero gives his power away, catalyst for chaos in the kingdom, suffers mental torment and chaos.	• Due to her honesty she is rejected by her father. • an innocent who is unlawfully murdered by Edmond
Actions and interactions that result in their death	• division of kingdom • belief in Goneril and Regan • banishment of Cordelia • madness	• refusal to pander to father • return to England to rescue Lear and reclaim his kingdom • Edmond's evil
Tragic flaw	• pride, arrogance • lack of self-knowledge • foolishness	• stubbornness

Impact of actions on plot	• kingdom in chaos • Kent banished	• her return to England with an army forces war
Impact of death on plot/other characters	• Last dramatic event in a catalogue of deaths in the final scene, Kent seeks to follow ear. • Edgar attempts to restore kingdom to order.	• Her death breaks Lear's heart, he dies.
Impact of death on audience	• Shakespeare presents Lear's torment in totality, his death is the final pinnacle of the tragedy.	• Her death is not shown on stage, Lear enters carrying her body. • Recognise her loyalty and love for Lear, she dies an innocent as a result of Lear's initial tragic flaw.
Judgement and analysis	• We have seen Lear's journey throughout the play, from egotistical ruler to embittered old man, left with nothing but his grief and regret. The loyalty of other characters prompts our loyalty to Lear, who achieves redemption through Cordelia's forgiveness.	• Cordelia is absent for much of the play, the focus is on Lear's tragedy. It is her forgiveness of and attempt to save her father that is her most powerful and dramatic act in the play.

Drama Toolbox

remind yourself of the definitions of different dramatic genres in AS in a Week pages 21, 22

2 **Relationships between texts: understanding the genre of drama**

Examiners want to see that you can 'explore and comment on relationships and comparisons between texts'.

This assessment objective is best met by:

- understanding the definition of the genre

- applying the definition to the particular play you are studying.

For example, William Congreve's *The Way of the World* is a Restoration comedy. The genre of Restoration comedy commonly employs the following features:

- Comedy of manners; plot is based on the deception of foolish characters by clever, witty characters.

- Characters are aristocratic.

- Characters struggle for sex, power and money.

- The dramatist exposes their seemingly sophisticated behaviour as artificial.

- Love is usually dealt with cynically rather than romantically, but a marriage is a common resolution.

- The comedy arises from the witty wordplay in the dialogue.

3 Assessment Objective 3 requires you to show a 'detailed understanding of the way in which writers' choice of form, structure and language shape meaning'.

Form

This is where you look at the type of drama you are studying. The key point here is to be able to say why the dramatist has chosen a particular form and how selection of form contributes to the meaning of the play.

A number of forms are offered below with comments about the possible effect they could have on the audience's response.

- Is it in verse?

Verse is often spoken by characters of status in a play. Verse in comedy – especially for mockery or bawdy purposes – is often more effective than prose.

- Is it in prose?

Prose is often the form of dialogue of the lower classes or used for persuasive speech.

- Is there a mixture of verse and prose?

A character that employs both verse and prose is presenting differing aspects of their personality, an ability to adapt to a variety of social situations, for example.

- Does the dramatist include songs?

Songs often offer relief and entertainment at pivotal points in the plot.

- Are there soliloquies?

- Are the soliloquies public or private?

A dramatist who selects a character to openly address the audience (public soliloquy) engages and involves the audience in their motivations and actions. Often an audience will find such a character charming or enticing. A dramatist who selects a character to convey their internal thoughts aloud (private soliloquy) is offering the audience important psychological insight into the dilemmas of the character.

- Are there asides?

A character is who is given an aside establishes a relationship with the audience and offers an alternative viewpoint on the main action of the play, often creating either sympathy or humour.

Structure

This is where you look at the organisation of the plot. You need to show the examiner that you appreciate why the dramatist has organised the action of the play in a certain way.

Language

This is where you show that you can interpret the dialogue in the play.

You learnt in *AS English in a Week* that drama employs conventions and that you must suspend your disbelief. Asides and soliloquies that are public and private are all examples of conventions in dramatic language.

Drama Toolbox

Following are some tips for reading drama to help you understand the text:

- Remember that dramatists write for an audience who are watching the play on stage, not for readers.

- In order for an audience to keep track of the dialogue, dramatists often employ patterns, using particular rhythms and repetitions of words and phrases.

- Different styles of dialogue are called registers.

- Read the play aloud to appreciate the tone, rhythm, imagery, movement and structure.

- Take a speech from your drama text and highlight two words from each line that are the most important. Actors will often place stress on these words to emphasise their importance. Read the speech aloud to see how this works in practice. You will find that the logic of a difficult speech becomes clear.

4 Assessment objective 4 requires you to be able to 'articulate independent opinions and judgements, informed by different interpretations of literary texts by other readers'. This means that you must have your own opinion, be prepared to justify it with evidence from the text and also be able to respond to alternative opinions and judgements.

You should always:

- break down the statement in the question

- consider the merits and the flaws of the statement in the question

- assert your own opinion of the text in relation to the statement in the question.

The best way to revise for fulfilling this assessment objective is to remember that there are always alternative interpretations of the drama text to the one you have. An interpretation is influenced by social, cultural and contextual positions. Consider *The Merchant of Venice* by William Shakespeare, for example. In his time there was a negative attitude to money-lenders and this would have obviously influenced the first audience's reaction to Shylock. A modern audience would be more receptive to the treatment of Shylock in the play as we do not

study the footnotes, endnotes or glossary provided in your drama text to make sense of vocabulary that has changed over time

remember TRIMS

the examiner is interested in your evaluation of the text, so be confident. Back up your ideas with evidence to show how you arrived at your viewpoint

hold the same social concerns. As Shylock is a Jew, how do you imagine an audience seeing the play just after the Second World War would have reacted? When you are considering the merits and flaws of any opinion you must be careful to place it in its appropriate cultural, historical and social context.

5 Assessment objective 5ii requires you to appreciate the 'significance of cultural, historical and contextual influences' on the literary texts you are studying.

Cultural influences

Consider carefully who the original audience would have been for the drama text you are studying. Shakespeare and his contemporaries' audiences were made up from a diverse range of social classes, as theatre was an inexpensive form of entertainment and easily accessible. Cultural influences change through time and have a direct impact on interpretation.

Historical influences

You need to show the examiner that you appreciate what was happening at the time of the play's original performance. For example, Shakespeare's *King Lear* was written at a time of major political controversy as King James proposed the unification of Scotland and England. King Lear's decision to divide the kingdom would have had vital resonance for the contemporary audience. The Jacobean view of Roman Catholic Italy is vital for an appreciation of John Webster's *The Duchess of Malfi*. Webster's audience viewed Italy as a land of sophisticated, aberrant corruption, luxury and evil; this helps us to understand why most of the characters in the play view the Duchess as headstrong and immorally lustful. Today we would perhaps view her as independent in her refusal to choose a husband, without regard for social class or the wishes of her family.

Contextual influences

You need to place the drama text you are studying in context, which means you need to gain an understanding of what other dramatists were producing at the time when your play was produced.

learn more about statement-based questions in the Drama Examination Question Toolbox chapter

use an encyclopedia or a guide to literature to research cultural, historic and social influences. Read the editor's introduction to the text.

120 minutes

Use your knowledge

Using your drama text, answer the following questions on the plot of the play. You will have the opportunity to attempt an examination question on your drama text in the Mock Examination section at the end of the book.

1 Why are the act and scenes divided in the way that they are?

2 How does the play begin?

3 How do the main themes develop?

4 How do the characters develop?

5 What do the characters expect?

6 Does the dramatist fulfil or deny the expectations of the characters and the audience?

7 What does the audience expect to happen?

8 How are the issues in the play resolved?

9 Are there any unresolved issues?

Drama Application

60 minutes

Test your knowledge

Study the following extract from William Shakespeare's *Othello* and answer the questions based on the assessment objectives that you have learnt about in the Drama Toolbox chapter.

Othello is a Moor who has become a general in the Venetian army, and has secretly married Desdemona. Iago, whom Othello believes to be 'utterly loyal and honest', has successfully schemed to make Othello believe that Desdemona has been unfaithful to him.

5.2 Enter Othello with a light. (He draws back a curtain, revealing)
Desdemona asleep in her bed.
OTHELLO:

1   *It is the cause, it is the cause, my soul.*
2   *Let me not name it to you, you chaste stars.*
3   *It is the cause. Yet I'll not shed her blood,*
4   *Nor scar that whiter skin of hers than snow,*
5   *And smooth as monumental alabaster.*
6   *Yet she must die, else she'll betray more men.*
7   *Put out the light, and then put out the light.*
8   *If I quench thee, thou flaming minister,*
9   *I can again thy former light restore*
10   *Should I repent me; but once put out thy light,*
11   *Thou cunning'st pattern of excelling nature,*
12   *I know not where is that Promethean heat*
13   *That can thy light relume. When I have picked thy rose*
14   *I cannot give it vital growth again.*
15   *It needs must wither. I'll smell thee on the tree. (He kisses her.)*
16   *O balmy breath, that dost almost persuade*
17   *Justice to break her sword! One more, one more.*
18   *Be thus when thou art dead, and I will kill thee*
19   *And love thee after. One more, and that's the last. (He kisses her.)*
20   *So sweet was ne'er so fatal. I must weep,*
21   *But they are cruel tears. This sorrow's heavenly,*
22   *It strikes where it doth love. She wakes.*

Drama Application

In the extract, Shakespeare presents Othello as a man who is determined to kill his wife and will feel no guilt as a result of his actions. His hatred for Desdemona is clear as he gathers the courage to kill her and is clearly able to justify this act for the good of mankind. How far do you agree with this view?

 Order the following plan into a suitably coherent response to the question above.

- One of his reasons for killing Desdemona is 'else she will betray more men.'

- He does not hate Desdemona as he says he will 'love thee' after describing her with celestial imagery.

- Othello does not gather courage but demonstrates his fatal capacity for self-deception to justify his intended actions.

- Othello is not determined: he wavers throughout this speech.

- The line 'Should I repent me' suggests that he is not convinced of his feelings and therefore is unsure as to whether he will feel guilt.

 The genre of the extract is tragedy because it has the following features:

- Othello is the eponym of the play (his name is the title).

- Jealousy is his tragic flaw.

- His murder of Desdemona is unjust as she is innocent.

- The climax of the play is when Othello's fatal mistake prompts him to kill himself.

 Label the following essay points to show whether they relate mostly to form, structure or language.

(a) It is appropriate that Othello's speech is in blank verse and poetic as this section of the play is satiated with his personal quandary, intensely tragic and emotive.

(b) The speech is divided into four sections, representing Othello's psychological insecurity in his decision to kill Desdemona.

(c) In the first section, lines 1 to 5, Othello uses imagery to describe Desdemona's purity.

(d) The repeated phrases such as 'It is the cause, it is the cause,' and 'Put out the light, and then put out the light' and 'One more, one more' convey Othello's passion and his attempt to convince himself to murder Desdemona.

(e) The paradoxes in lines 20 and 21 convey Othello's vacillation and the extremes of his emotions induced by preparing to kill the one he loves.

(f) The second section, lines 6 to 15, uses images of fire to represent sexual desire and passion, as Othello believes Iago's machinations which imply that Desdemona has been unfaithful to him.

(g) In the first section, Othello evokes Desdemona's beauty using images of purity.

4 State key points of the essay title.

5 The text was written in 1604. Label the following points to state whether they relate to cultural, historical or contextual influences.

(a) Shakespeare's decision to make a black man a tragic hero was audacious and inventive.

(b) As blackness was by ancient tradition associated with sin and death, black Moors were generally villainous.

(c) *Othello* was very successful in Shakespeare's time and was one of the first plays to be acted after the theatres reopened in 1660.

(d) In this extract, Othello acts as judge and executioner, demonstrating his domination of Desdemona and reflecting the power and control men had over women in Shakespeare's time.

Answers

See Drama Application Improve your Knowledge pages 24–28 for answers.

✔ **If you got them all right, skip to page 29**

45 minutes

Improve your knowledge

1 An essay plan needs to be logical and coherent. Look at the comments on the essay plan from the Test your knowledge section. You will be asked to mark your own essay plans using the Assessment Objective (AO1).

Key points from AS in a Week
Drama Application pages 28–36

(a) Othello is not determined: he wavers throughout this speech.

(b) The line 'Should I repent me' suggests that he is not convinced of his feelings and therefore is unsure as to whether he will feel guilt.

(c) He does not hate Desdemona as he says he will 'love thee' after describing her with celestial imagery.

(d) Othello does not gather courage but demonstrates his fatal capacity for self-deception to justify his intended actions.

(e) One of his reasons for killing Desdemona is 'else she will betray more men'.

Most importantly, this essay plan methodically follows the structure of the question and also responds to the key points with evidence from the text. When you are marking your own essay plan to see whether it is coherent, try to relate each point back to the question. If you have incorporated phrases from the question, then you can be certain you are making relevant points.

2 Genre

It is important to understand the features of genre and apply them to your own text. Remind yourself of the example used in the Drama Toolbox on page 14.

Key points for applying them to your own text is to revise the definitions of the genres and see which one fits your play best. Remember that some plays, such as Shakespeare's *Measure for Measure* and *Troilus and Cressida* employ features of several genres and are commonly known as 'problem plays'.

An excellent way of improving your understanding of genre is to read, view or see performed other plays of the same genre. Look at the following table for alternative plays of common genres.

many plays can be viewed on video, or listened to on audiotape or CD. Town libraries, bookshops and even some of the high street music stores can prove to be very helpful

Drama Application

Genre	Examples
Problem play	*A Doll's House* Henrik Ibsen *Mrs Warren's Profession* George Bernard Shaw *All's Well That Ends Well* William Shakespeare
Comedy of manners	*Love's Labours Lost* William Shakespeare *Much Ado About Nothing* William Shakespeare *The Way of the World* William Congreve *The Rivals* Richard Sheridan *A School for Scandal* Richard Sheridan
History or chronicle play	*Edward II* Christopher Marlowe *Julius Caesar* William Shakespeare *A Man for All Seasons* Robert Bold *Richard II, Henry IV Parts I and II, Henry V* William Shakespeare
Romantic comedy	*As You Like It* William Shakespeare *A Midsummer Night's Dream* William Shakespeare
Tragedy	*The Spanish Tragedy* Thomas Kyd *The Jew Of Malta* Christopher Marlowe *The Duchess of Malfi, The White Devil* Christopher Marlowe *Death of a Salesman* Arthur Miller *Murder in the Cathedral* TS Eliot *Salome* Oscar Wilde
Satiric comedy	*The Country Wife* William Wycherley *The Threepenny Opera* Bertolt Brecht *The Alchemist* Ben Jonson *The Misanthrope* Molière *Arms and the Man* George Bernard Shaw *The Importance of Being Ernest* Oscar Wilde *An Ideal Husband* Oscar Wilde

Drama Application

This assessment objective is about form, structure and language. Look at the examiner's comments in the boxes on the essay points from Test your knowledge.

Student is able to identify the form of the extract. Shows how the form has an effect on the meaning. Is able to incorporate three key points, which refer to Othello, to the genre and to the response of the audience.

- It is appropriate that Othello's speech is in blank verse and poetic as this section of the play is satiated with his personal quandary, intensely tragic and emotive.

- The speech is divided into four sections representing Othello's psychological insecurity in his decision to kill Desdemona.

- The first section, lines 1 to 5, Othello uses imagery to describe Desdemona's purity.

- The repeated phrases such as 'It is the cause, it is the cause' and 'Put out the light, and then put out the light' and 'One more, one more' convey Othello's passion and his attempt to convince himself to murder Desdemona.

- The paradoxes in lines 20 and 21 convey Othello's vacillation and the extremes of his emotions induced by preparing to kill the one he loves.

- The second section, lines 6 to 15, uses images of fire to represent sexual desire and passion as Othello believes Iago's machinations which suggest that Desdemona has been unfaithful to him.

- In the first section, Othello evokes Desdemona's beauty using images of purity.

Student effectively summarises the movement of the speech and is able to show how the structure of Othello's speech shapes the meaning. I will be interested to see if the student is able to identify the nature of the four sections to support this statement.

Excellent attention to the language, the student uses the appropriate literary term, analyses the meaning and is able to say what the paradox conveys about Othello.

Good, the student has developed the second point. I would like to see embedded quotations in the essay and analysis of the language.

Drama Application

Key point of essay	Student's opinion	Examiner's comments
4 Othello is determined to kill his wife.	He lacks the conviction to kill Desdemona and has to persuade himself that to murder her will be just and right. The vacillation is evident in the structure of the speech as he moves to stating that he will 'not shed her blood' and elevates her using celestial imagery in lines 1 to 5, reflecting on her passion which he believes resulted in her adultery and rebellion of her fidelity to him from line 6 to 15, is swayed by her beauty in lines 16 to 19, and finally resolves himself to the act in a catalogue of paradoxes in lines 20 to 22. He is, however, determined that Desdemona has betrayed him.	This student has clearly and effectively identified the structure of the speech, analysed the progression of Othello's psychological torment and has made focused comments based on textual evidence. A successful response to the statement as the final comment redirects the question of 'determination' to a more appropriate idea. A complete and thorough response to the statement.
Will feel no guilt as a result of his actions.	Othello promotes himself to the status of judge and executioner through the use of imperatives in 'she must die' and believes that through executing her, he is redeeming her and restoring her 'former light.' However, the line 'Should I repent me' conveys to the audience his insecurity about his elevated position and hence we cannot be convinced that he will feel no guilt as he deliberates throughout the speech. Moreover, he is almost swayed out of his role by her breath and the kiss as he exclaims 'that dost almost persuade/ Justice to break her sword!'.	Clearly articulates perceptive independent opinions particularly in the comment about Othello's view that he is 'judge and executioner'. This demonstrates the student is able to offer an independent critical position. I would be looking to see if the student develops this point throughout the essay. The student has evaluated the interpretation.
His hatred for Desdemona is clear.	Othello offers diverse feelings about Desdemona through the use of contrasting imagery and colour. In the first section he uses hyperbolic imagery, 'whiter skin of hers than snow, / And smooth as monumental alabaster' and later compares her to images of nature such as a rose. The paradoxes of the final section of the speech clearly demonstrate his internal turmoil at killing the beautiful object of his own desire and love.	Through key textual references the student has refuted the interpretation in the question and offered a convincing and sophisticated judgement of the section of the text.

Drama Application

Gathers the courage to kill her.	It is not courage that Othello gathers throughout the speech but will-power that derives from his belief in Desdemona's infidelity. He continues to convince himself by becoming the representative of justice.	*Again, clear response to the statement and extended by offering an alternative viewpoint. This links effectively with the student's previous comments about Othello's capacity for self-deception.*
Othello is clearly able to justify this act for the good of mankind.	Othello is a master of self-deception and through the reference to 'Justice's sword' he convinces himself that he is acting for the good of man, to redeem her nature through execution and extinguish the fire that is a metaphor for Desdemona's unnatural desire and passion for another man.	*The student demonstrates understanding of Othello as a character and is able to pinpoint how his tragic flaw is revealed in the extract. The agreement with the key point is evident but it is also extended to incorporate Othello's belief that his murder of Desdemona will restore her spiritually.*

5 Look at the examiner's comments on the student's response to question 5 of the Test your knowledge section.

Student demonstrates awareness of contemporary responses to the text and the status of the theatre in the seventeenth century.

- Shakespeare's decision to make a black man a tragic hero was audacious and inventive.

- As blackness was by ancient tradition associated with sin and death, black Moors were generally villainous.

- *Othello* was very successful in Shakespeare's time and was one of the first plays to be acted after the theatres reopened in 1660.

- In this extract Othello acts as judge and executioner, demonstrating his domination of Desdemona and reflecting the power and control men had over women in Shakespeare's time.

Student shows awareness of a feminist perspective on the text.

Student needs to develop this statement to show how the audience responds to Othello throughout the play. Are we eventually sympathetic or do we finally condemn him?

Detailed knowledge is evident and the student will need to progress and evaluate the effect of the statement on the play.

Drama Application

60 minutes

Use your knowledge

1 Using your drama text, think up as many different types of questions as you can and in 15 minutes write an essay plan for each. Write a paragraph to explain the generic features of the drama you are studying and how the dramatist has either followed the dramatic conventions of the genre or been unconventional.

2 Write a paragraph to explain the dramatist's treatment of each of the following terms for the drama texts you are studying: form, structure and language.

3 Think up as many statements about the drama text you are studying as you can. Remember you don't have to agree with them. Then, write a paragraph for each statement evaluating the statement and asserting your own relevant opinion.

4 Write a paragraph for each of the following influences for the drama text you are studying: cultural, historical and contextual.

Drama Question Examination Toolbox

20 minutes

Test your knowledge

As an A-level English literature student you should feel confident tackling any type of question on the drama texts you have studied. This chapter revises the tools you need to answer commonly asked examination questions on drama texts.

Here is a list of five sample examination questions. Label the sample examination questions as:

(a) character-based

(b) statement-based

(c) close extract-based

(d) thematic based

(e) audience response-based

(f) genre-based.

1 It has been said that the tragedy in *Othello* is a result of the lovers, Othello and Desdemona, never knowing each other. How far do you agree with this statement or are there other reasons that can be attributed to the tragic outcome?

2 In *Measure for Measure* Shakespeare explores the topic of justice and morality. Select appropriate extracts from the play to demonstrate Shakespeare's treatment of this topic.

3 'The presentation of evil is appealing because Volpone and Mosca are such charismatic characters whereas Bonario and Celia, who embody goodness, are simply tame and uninteresting.' How far do you agree with the critic's assessment of Ben Jonson's play?

Drama Question Examination Toolbox

4 'The struggle in Oscar Wilde's *The Importance of Being Ernest* is the conflict between the force to behave unnaturally as demanded by social convention and the inclination to behave according to natural desires.' Is this an appropriate and accurate view of the play?

5 Remind yourself of scene 10, lines 1 to 62 in *Dr Faustus*. This scene is often omitted from editions and performances because it is low comedy and adds nothing to the play. Could you justify its inclusion?

6 A Restoration version of *King Lear* by Nahum Tate altered the plot and allowed Lear, Cordelia and Gloucester to survive. It was thought that the ending of the play was too horrific and catastrophic for an audience. Discuss the advantages and disadvantages of presenting Nahum Tate's version of *King Lear*.

Answers

 If you got them all right, skip to page 35

45 minutes

Improve your knowledge

1 A genre-based question will ask you to consider the genre of the play you are studying and how the dramatist conforms to or undermines the convention of the genre. When you answering this type of question focus on the following:

- List the generic features.

- Select examples from the text to show how each feature is presented.

- Consider plot, character, setting and use of language in your answer.

- Incorporate other relevant texts you have studied in the same genre.

2 When you are answering a question based on a theme in the drama you are studying, focus on the following:

Presentation of the theme (plot)

- At which point in the play is the theme introduced?

- How does it develop?

- How is the theme resolved?

Characters' involvement

- Which characters are involved in the theme?

- How are the characters affected by the theme?

Use of language

- Are there particular images or phrases associated with the theme?

- Does the dramatist use metaphors or similes when referring to the theme?

A character-based question will ask you to consider how well the characters fit a particular statement, or even ask you to compare two different characters and their approaches to life. When you are answering this type of question focus on the following:

- How is the character constructed?

- What significant actions do they enact?

- What are the motivations for their actions?

- How do their actions affect the plot?

- How do their actions affect other characters?

- What type of language do they use?

remember FRAISIER from AS in a Week p23

 Students often struggle with statement-based questions. Remember that the examiner is keen to read your insights into and interpretations of the play. When answering this type of question focus on the following:

- Define the words used and divide the elements of the statement into parts.

- Consider each part of the statement in turn.

- Choose extracts of the play that could be used to respond to this statement.

- Apply each extract to the statement and evaluate how true the statement is in light of the text.

- Offer your own opinion of the statement – does it leave anything out?

remember relevance: answer the statement, do not give an overall assessment of the play

Drama Question Examination Toolbox

 A close scene analysis question will always ask you to focus in on the extract offered and require you to place the extract in the context of the play. When answering this type of question focus on the following:

- What is the specific angle the question is asking you to consider in the extract?

- How does the extract reveal, support or contradict the statement that is offered?

- Construct a close critical analysis of the language of the extract with the question in mind.

- What is important in the extract and where it occurs in the play?

 An audience-based question will ask you to consider the impact of the drama on an audience.

When answering this type of question consider the following:

- How does the dramatist manipulate our responses?

- Do our feelings change towards the characters during the course of the play?

- What does the audience expect to happen? Does the dramatist fulfil or deny those expectations?

remember relevance

think about the dramatic structure of the play

re-read the play in one sitting to gain an experience similar to the audience and jot down your responses as you visualise the play being performed

Drama Question Examination Toolbox

20 minutes

Use your knowledge

1 A genre-based question will ask me to consider how the play I am studying fits into the genre. I will need to understand the generic _____ and discuss how the dramatist has _____ those features in the play I am studying.

2 A thematic-based question will ask me to look at how the _____ is presented, developed and _____ throughout the play. I will need to look at the _____ of the plot, the _____ involvement in the theme and the _____ associated with the theme.

3 A character-based question will ask me to look at how the character is _____ , to consider the character's actions, _____ and _____ in the drama. I will also need to analyse carefully the character' use of _____ and their contribution to the _____ of the play.

4 A statement-based question will provide me with an _____ of the play I am studying. I will need to _____ that statement to see how far I think it applies to the play and also offer my own _____ .

5 A close scene analysis question will either _____ me with an extract(s) or ask me to _____ an extract(s) from the play I am studying and require me to state how far I agree with the statement they have given. I should also consider how the extract fits into the _____ as a whole.

6 An audience-based question will ask me to consider the _____ of the audience and to discuss the _____ the dramatist uses to the audience's responses.

20 minutes

Test your knowledge

1 The plot of a novel is shaped so that the reader's _____ are raised and _____ is created.

2 Themes can be presented in an obvious way or in a subtle way. Give two terms which describe these alternative ways of presenting themes.

3 Name three ways in which an author may provide the reader with an indication of a character's personality.

4 Identify whether the narratorial voice in the following extract is first or third person:

Once upon a time and a very good time it was there was a moocow coming down along the road and this moocow that was coming down along the road met a nicens little boy named baby tuckoo…

His father told him that story: his father looked at him through a glass: he had a hairy face.

He was baby tuckoo. The moocow came down along the road where Betty Byrne lived: she sold lemon platt.

5 Choose the words that you feel correctly complete the following sentence.

Setting and environment are _____ (important/unimportant) in the portrayal of a novel. The environment _____ (has little to do with/can create) the atmosphere of a scene. The emotions of a character are _____ (never/sometimes/always) reflected by the setting.

Answers

1 expectations, suspense 2 explicit, implicit 3 any three of the following: by what they say, by what they do, through the description of their clothes, through a description of their physique or face, by how they speak, through what other people say about them, through what the narrator says about them 4 The narratorial voice is third person, but enters the child's mind and as a result, takes on his childish vocabulary (from *A Portrait of the Artist as a Young Man* by James Joyce). 5 important, can create, sometimes

✔ **If you got them all right, skip to page 40**

Prose Toolbox

30 minutes

Improve your knowledge

When you write about a novel, it is important to remember that it is the creation of the author. You should therefore always bear in mind that a writer has written a novel so that a reader will respond to it in a particular way.

Key points from AS in a Week

Prose Toolbox
pages 64–69

 1 **Structure and plot**

You should try to identify how the author raises expectation in the reader and creates suspense and excitement by manipulating the plot. It is important to identify at what point, and how, the author relieves the tension and suspense; don't forget that surprise is an important technique in keeping the plot interesting. There are various different types of plot:

- plots dominated by events that took place before the novel started

- plots that are directed by a character who wishes to achieve a goal

- plots that describe the life and experiences of a central character

- plots based on a character's discovery

- plots that explore the workings of society

- plots based on a mystery.

write a brief summary of the plot

2 **Theme**

The theme concerns the ideas that are presented either explicitly, or more often, implicitly, in the novel. Some themes occur in many novels, like love, conflict, and revenge. When you are writing about a novel, you should consider how you feel the author approaches the themes. A first step should be to ask yourself why a novel has been given its title – the author may be disclosing to the reader something important about the novel.

Symbols, especially repeated ones, can be important in enhancing or highlighting a theme. The way the novel's plot has been constructed or ordered can also be an expression of the themes. Sometimes themes are identified by important speeches which focus on the main concerns of the plot. Events, particularly climaxes, also help highlight themes.

record your first impressions of the novel

 ### Characterisation

Characterisation is achieved by directly telling the reader what the character thinks and by exposing us to their words and actions. The author will not always do this directly – it may be through the clothes that the character wears, how they speak, react or think.

When you want to write about a character it is useful to select several passages from the novel that you feel highlight key aspects of the character. You will find that some characters are rich and complex, and change and grow through the novel. Others are shallow and straightforward and rarely surprise the reader. Often, such characters add to the action or plot of the novel and therefore a well-defined character is not so important. Novelists therefore create a very wide range of characters in terms of their fullness. Always keep your mind open to the fact that even the most fixed character may change through the novel.

 ### Narratorial voice

In *AS English in a Week*, we identified that there are two types of narrator. First person narrators are involved indirectly or directly with the events of the novel and, as characters themselves, can be either reliable or unreliable. Third person narrators do not participate in the events but tell the story, either as an outside observer (objective) or as a narrator who is all-knowing and can tell the reader about the characters' thoughts and about events happening at the same time in different places (omniscient) or as a narrator who offers moral judgement on the characters (intrusive).

read and write as much as possible

Using a first person narrator allows the author to achieve several effects. Firstly, we feel very close to the narrator as we share their thoughts and feelings and experience events with them, knowing only what they know. Therefore, when the narrator is confused by events we often share that confusion. Sometimes, however, the author creates irony by allowing the reader to understand events that the narrator does not. For example, Leo in *The Go-Between*, surrounded by Victorian austerity, does not guess, as the reader quickly does, that the messages he takes between Ted, the local farmer, and Marian who lives at the Hall, are not merely 'business letters'.

First person narration allows the reader to understand how the narrator thinks and therefore for emotions to be shared. It allows a reader to see how the world looks to someone else and to observe how the narrator grows and changes through the novel. Third person narrators are very powerful because they can order events as they please and access any character's mind. Sometimes a narrator has access to only one of the characters' minds and in this way allows the reader to see all that one character thinks and feels – a little like a first person narration.

 ## 5 Setting and environment

The setting of a novel helps to create atmosphere, mood and feeling. A landscape can reflect a character's emotions and therefore you should try to draw a comparison between the two. Consider how a particular setting or series of settings points to the theme of the novel. Settings are not incidental, but a significant part of the novel as a whole. Focus closely on the language used in the description.

always re-read your novel – you miss key aspects first time around

Prose Toolbox

45 minutes

Use your knowledge

Thinking carefully about your set novel, answer the following questions.

1 Look closely at the structure of the plot. How has the author created suspense or tension through the plot and how is the reader's expectation created?

2 Is there a repeated symbol in your novel and what is its significance to the theme or themes of the novel?

3 Identify the main characters in the novels that you are studying. Examine each one to establish how deep and detailed the portrayal is. Consider carefully why the author has created them in this way.

4 Identify whether the narrator of the novel is first or third person. How does this affect the presentation of events and the reader's response to and interpretation of the plot?

5 What does the setting reveal about the personality or situation of the characters or the themes of the novel?

Pre-1900 Prose Application

60 minutes

Test your knowledge

Read the extract from *Wuthering Heights* by Emily Brontë, published in 1847. Write a paragraph, using evidence from the extract, for each of the following:

1 Brontë's style and use of literary devices

2 The type of novel you think it is

3 (a) The form of the extract
(b) The structure of the extract
(c) The language used in the extract

4 An evaluation of the following statement: 'This extract demonstrates Brontë's concern with how the external environment mirrors character.'

5 Brontë's exploration of cultural, social and historical contexts.

1   *Wuthering Heights is the name of Mr Heathcliff's dwelling. 'Wuthering' being a*
2   *significant provincial adjective, descriptive of the atmospheric tumult to which its*
3   *station is exposed in stormy weather. Pure, bracing ventilation they must have up*
4   *there at all times, indeed: one may guess the power of the north wind, blowing*
5   *over the edge, by the excessive slant of a few stunted firs at the end of the*
6   *house; and by a range of gaunt thorns all stretching their limbs one way, as if*
7   *craving the alms of the sun. Happily, the architect had the foresight to build it*
8   *strong: the narrow windows are deeply set in the wall, and the corners defended*
9   *with large jutting stones.*

10   *Before passing the threshold, I paused to admire a quantity of grotesque carving*
11   *lavished over the front, and especially about the principal door, above which,*
12   *among a wilderness of crumbling griffins, and shameless little boys, I detected*
13   *the date '1500,' and the name 'Hareton Earnshaw'. I would have made a few*
14   *comments, and requested the history of the place, from the surly owner, but his*
15   *attitude at the door appeared to demand my speedy entrance, or complete*
16   *departure, and I had no desire to aggravate his impatience, previous to*
17   *inspecting the penetralium.*

18   *One step brought us into the family sitting-room, without any introductory lobby,*
19   *or passage: they call it here 'the house' pre-eminently. It includes the kitchen,*
20   *and the parlour, generally, but I believe at Wuthering Heights the kitchen is*
21   *forced to retreat altogether into another quarter, at least I distinguished a chatter*
22   *of tongues, and a clatter of culinary utensils, deep within; and I observed no*
23   *signs of roasting, boiling, or baking, about the huge fire-place; nor any glitter of*
24   *copper saucepans and tin cullenders on the walls. One end, indeed, reflected*
25   *splendidly both light and heat, from ranks of immense pewter dishes,*
26   *interspersed with silver jugs and tankards, towering row after row, in a vast oak*
27   *dresser to the very roof. The latter had never been underdrawn, its entire*
28   *anatomy laid bare to an inquiring eye, expect where a frame of wood laden with*
29   *oatcakes, and clusters of legs of beef, mutton, and ham concealed it. Above the*
30   *chimney were sundry villainous old guns, and a couple of horse-pistols, and, by*
31   *way of ornament, three gaudily painted canisters disposed along its ledge. The*
32   *floor was of smooth, white stone: the chairs, high-backed primitive structures,*
33   *painted green: one or two heavy black ones lurking in the shade. In an arch,*
34   *under the dresser, reposed a huge, liver coloured bitch pointer surrounded by a*
35   *swarm of squealing puppies; and other dogs haunted the recesses.*

36 The apartment and furniture would have been nothing extraordinary as
37 belonging to a homely, northern farmer with a stubborn countenance, and
38 stalwart limbs, set out to advantage in knee-breeches, and gaiters. Such an
39 individual, seated in his armchair, his mug of ale frothing on the round table
40 before him, is to be seen in any circuit of five or six miles among these hills, if
41 you go at the right time, after dinner. But, Mr Heathcliff forms a singular contrast
42 to his abode and style of living. He is a dark skinned gypsy, in aspect, in dress,
43 and manners a gentleman, that is, as much a gentleman as many a country
44 squire: rather slovenly, perhaps, yet not looking amiss with his negligence,
45 because he has an erect and handsome figure, and rather morose; possibly, some
46 people might suspect him of a degree of underbred pride – I have a sympathetic
47 chord within that tells me it is nothing of the sort; I know, by instinct, his reserve
48 springs from an aversion to showy displays of feeling – to manifestations of
49 mutual kindness. He'll love and hate, equally under cover, and esteem it a
50 species of impertinence, to be loved or hated again – No, I'm running on too fast
51 – I bestow my own attributes over liberally on him. Mr Heathcliff may have
52 entirely dissimilar reasons for keeping his hand out of the way, when he meets a
53 would be acquaintance, to those which actuate me. Let me hope my
54 constitution is almost peculiar: my dear mother used to say I should never have a
55 comfortable home, and only last summer, I proved myself perfectly unworthy of
56 one.

Answers

You could almost refer to sections of the extract as textual evidence. It is important that you are able to refer to specific sections of the text and write about them in a focused way. Compare your paragraphs with the paragraphs written by a student in the Improve your knowledge section.

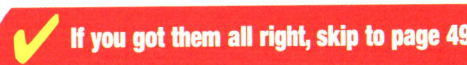
✔ If you got them all right, skip to page 49

60 minutes

Improve your knowledge

1 It is important that you are able to evaluate the writer's use of language using appropriate literary terms. From this you can develop an overview of the writer's style. This is an extremely useful approach to apply to your own pre-1900 text. The bleak moorlands in Yorkshire where she grew up heavily influenced Emily Brontë. The first paragraph reflects this:

In the first paragraph Brontë depicts a powerful north wind that has a devastating affect on the surroundings and provides a suitably tragic and desolate environment for the tragedy to follow. The use of 'exposed' 'excessive slant of a few stunted firs', and a 'range of gaunt thorns all stretching their limbs one way, as if craving the alms of the sun' effectively denotes an environment which lacks warmth, light and nurturing, essential elements for growth. Brontë uses the landscape as a metaphor for the characters that suffer as a result of Heathcliff's passion. Hence, the north wind could be a metaphor for Heathcliff who is a powerful man and has a dramatic effect upon all those who come into contact with him.

Key points from AS in a Week

Pre-1900 Prose Application
            pages 70–74

remember to have a dictionary to look up words that you are unfamiliar with

2 ## Types of Victorian novels

Novels in the Victorian period ranged from romantic, Gothic, realist, dramatic, melodramatic, sensational, agnostic, those conveying social concerns, mystery and history genres or even a mixture of types.

Type of novel	Common features	Examples
Romantic	Emphasis on imagination and feeling over logical thought, belief that humans are by nature good, that Nature, as in the external environment, weather and seasons, is the source of divine feeling. An understanding of romanticism is important to appreciate its contrast with realism.	Mostly applied to poets such as Wordsworth, Coleridge and Byron but also influenced writers such as Jane Austen.

Gothic	General mood is that of decay, the action is dramatic, violent and unsettling, love is usually passionate but destructive and the environments are like that of the medieval world including a use of architectural settings that are flamboyant, mysterious, grotesque or even frightening.	Emily Brontë's *Wuthering Heights*, Charlotte Brontë's *Jane Eyre*, Henry James' *The Turn of the Screw*, Mary Shelley's *Frankenstein*.
Realistic	Represents plot, characters and setting that are in line with the reader's perception of the world. Characters are depicted in detail and are well developed throughout the novel. Their interactions are credible. The setting is in a specific environment and historical time period. Writers of realist novels seek to provide credible psychological insight for motivations of the characters.	George Eliot's *The Mill on the Floss*, Henry James' *The Portrait of a Lady*, Stephen Crane's *A Girl Called Maggie*, Elizabeth Gaskell's *Mary Barton*.
Melodramatic	The conflict is between pure good and pure evil, where the heroes and/or heroines are moral and upright but are threatened and troubled by contemptible villains. The situations are often improbable and stock elements are used to evoke a emotional range of pity and terror from the audience.	Alexander Dumas' *The Count of Monte Cristo*. This is generally a pejorative term and is often parodied in literature. Charles Dickens' *Oliver Twist* pokes fun at melodramas, although critics have called the novel a melodrama itself.
Social	The novel is concerned with the social and economic position of the characters, highlighting the inequality and injustice of the time. The novel seeks to advocate a change through the struggle of the characters, which is often fruitless.	Charles Dickens' *Bleak House* and *Hard Times*.
Agnostic	The key issue here is the deterioration of religious faith. The characters often find that their faith offers them little relief in a society that is indifferent to their outcome. Fate and destiny play key roles in the tragic events that follow.	Thomas Hardy's *Tess of The D'Urbervilles* and *Jude the Obscure*.

Now read the student's comments on *Wuthering Heights*.

The genre of the novel is realistic and tragic. This is evident from the continual use of conflicting images and issues that Brontë offers in the extract. The presentation of Heathcliff as a man who will both 'love and hate, equally under cover,' demonstrates that he is the central figure in the novel and that the passion of these emotions will have a powerful influence on the events and the characters that follow.

 3 (a) **Form**

Remember that this is the way the novel is conveyed to you. An important feature of *Wuthering Heights* is the shifting of narrative viewpoints. Mr Lockwood, an outsider, and Mrs Dean, a servant of the Earnshaw family, relate the novel. This increases suspense as we discover the history of the house with Mr Lockwood.

As this section of the novel is conveyed in the first person it offers the reader a personal insight on the title of the novel and of the main character Heathcliff. We are invited to view the place and the person through the eyes of Mr Lockwood who is detached from the events of the house as he does not know the history. This creates suspense as we, with Mr Lockwood, are invited to discover the secrets of the house and its inhabitants.

(b) **Structure**

It is always useful to know how the novel was originally serialised. Read your introduction thoroughly to gain this information. It will show you how the author divided the plot, creating suspense for readers to ensure that they bought the next issue.

re-read the Prose Toolbox chapter to help you identify the structure of the plot

Create your own plot line for the novel highlighting the significant changes in plot and the introduction, continuation and resolution of key themes.

The structure of the extract moves from an external depiction of environment surrounding the house, namely the hostile landscape. Within this tragic framework of hostile nature, through the eyes of the first person narrator, Brontë moves to a physical description of the house itself. The reader is consistently invited to view the dwelling through the eyes of the visitor. Brontë describes the external physical attributes of the house before moving to the internal. The hostile exterior is mirrored in the internal through the notable lack of domesticity, the references to objects in the 'shade' and the dogs that 'haunted the recesses'. This gives the extract an ominous atmosphere which is fulfilled in the description of Mr Heathcliff, who is finally described as discordant with his surroundings and of a passionate extreme nature.

(c) Language

First, ensure that you are equipped with a good dictionary, as many of the words of nineteenth century novels may be unfamiliar to you. Check your text for a glossary or notes in the back of the book that offer explanations of the more unusual words and phrases. Then you will have a sound knowledge of the language and be able to analyse the effects of the writer's use of language. Read the student's paragraph below as an example.

 When answering a statement-based question it is vital to evaluate the statement and be able to offer your own viewpoints. A productive way to plan answering a statement-based question is to:

- break down the statement, defining any unusual terms in your own words

- assess each component of the statement against the text, check whether there is evidence for this viewpoint

- offer your own judgement based on textual evidence.

Remember that you may find that you agree with some elements of the statement and disagree with others. The examiner wants to read your interpretations – remember, your views are just as valid as anyone else's as long as they are supported with evidence from the text and are relevant to the question.

The following is an example of an answer you could have written for question 4 in Test your knowledge.

In the extract Brontë uses pathetic fallacy to establish the bleak and sombre tone of the passage. This is further enhanced by the description of the house as being lavished with 'grotesque carving', 'a wilderness of crumbling griffins'. The notion of oppression is additionally significant as evident in the 'excessive slant of a few stunted firs', 'a range of gaunt thorns' in the external environment, subsequently mirrored in the description of the kitchen which 'is forced to retreat altogether into another quarter'. The feeling of foreboding is further continued in Brontë's personification of the 'villainous old guns' and the chairs that are described as 'lurking in the shade'. The delineation of Mr Heathcliff confirms our foreboding as he is depicted as aloof, 'rather morose' and subject to extremes of emotion. I agree with the statement that Brontë uses the external environment to mirror the character of Mr Heathcliff as we are encouraged to attribute the domestic situation that is lacking in life to his influence and link it to the hostility he shows to the visitor, the narrator.

5 Cultural, social and historical contexts

This is where you need to read the introduction to your novel and critical texts carefully. It is vital that you have an understanding of the writer, their time and any historical events that may have influenced their writing. Read the following student's paragraph as an example.

The detailed references to the domestic equipment represents that Wuthering Heights is a place of genuine domestic economy. In this extract the narrator remarks on how the kitchen is 'forced into retreat', how the dresser is 'exposed' and the lack of a noise, which reflect that the domesticity and security of cooking is absent. It indicates that a domestic environment is one that the author was familiar with and considered a central part of life.

Remember the definition of pathetic fallacy is where a writer attributes human characteristics to inanimate nature. It is a more specific description than personification, which covers a range of subjects such as synthetic materials, for example. Using the precise terminology will impress the examiner!

Pre-1900 Prose Application

60 minutes

Use your knowledge

Answer the questions below using your pre-1900 prose text.

1 Identify key literary terms that are appropriate to an evaluation of the text.

2 To which genre does the novel that you are studying belong?

3 Write a paragraph based on each of the following features:
(a) form
(b) structure
(c) language.

4 From a critical essay or the introduction to your text, identify a key statement and construct a question around it.

5 Using your pre-1900 prose text, write a paragraph on each of the following features:
(a) cultural influences
(b) historical influences
(c) contextual influences.

60 minutes

Test your knowledge

The following extract is from D H Lawrence's *Lady Chatterley's Lover*. Describe how Lawrence uses literary devices to convey the scene successfully and try to identify what, if any, twentieth century concerns are raised. You may wish to refer back to the Prose chapters in *AS English in a Week* before you start.

1   In spite of May and a new greenness, the country was dismal. It was rather chilly,
2   and there was smoke on the rain, and a certain sense of exhaust vapour in the
3   air. One just had to live from one's resistance. No wonder these people were ugly
4   and tough.

5   The car ploughed uphill through the long squalid straggle of Tevershall, the
6   blackened brick dwellings, the black slate roofs glistening their sharp edges, the
7   mud black with coal-dust, the pavements wet and black. It was as if dismalness
8   had soaked through and through everything. The utter negation of natural
9   beauty, the utter negation of the gladness of life, the utter absence of the instinct
10 for shapely beauty which every bird and beast has, the utter death of the human
11 intuitive faculty was appalling. The stacks of soap in the grocers' shops, the
12 rhubarb and lemons in the greengrocers! The awful hats in the milliners! All went
13 by ugly, ugly, ugly, followed by the plaster-and-gilt horror of the cinema with its
14 wet picture announcements, 'A Woman's Love!', and the new big Primitive chapel,
15 primitive enough in its stark brick and big panes of greenish and raspberry glass
16 in its stark windows. The Wesleyan chapel, higher up, was of blackened brick and
17 stood behind iron railings and blackened shrubs. The Congregational chapel,
18 which thought itself superior, was built of rusticated sandstone and had a steeple,
19 but not a very high one. Just beyond were the new school buildings, expensive
20 pink brick, and gravelled playground inside iron railings, all very imposing, and
21 mixing the suggestion of a chapel and a prison. Standard Five girls were having a
22 singing lesson, just finishing the la-me-do-la exercises and beginning a 'sweet
23 children's song'. Anything more unlike song, spontaneous song, would be
24 impossible to imagine: a strange bawling yell that followed the outlines of a tune.
25 It was not like savages: savages have subtle rhythms. It was not like animals:
26 animals mean something when they yell. It was like nothing on earth, and it was
27 called singing. Connie sat and listened with her heart in her boots, as Field was
28 filling petrol. What could possibly become of such a people, a people in whom the
29 living intuitive faculty was dead as nails, and only queer mechanical yells and
30 uncanny will-power remained?

Post-1900 Prose Application

30 minutes

Improve your knowledge

This extract describes the mining town of Tevershall as seen through the eyes of Connie Chatterley, the heroine of the novel. Critically examining a small passage from your novel can help you identify the themes, characterisation, narratorial voice, setting and literary devices used; this will help you link ideas with the rest of the novel and therefore enable you to take an incisive overall view of your text. This passage is used as an example and you should try to adopt the same approach with your own set texts.

Key points from AS in a Week

Post-1900 Prose Application
pages 75–78

read the text closely and carefully

Themes

The theme in this passage deals with the presentation of the miners through direct commentary and the description of the mining town. The miners are described as 'ugly and tough' (to Connie) having to live 'from one's resistance' due to their depressing lifestyle and surroundings. The commentary describes a people who have replaced sensitivity with determination and resolve. Lawrence uses a simile to illustrate this: 'People in whom the living intuitive faculty was dead as nails … and only … uncanny will-power remained'. This theme reflects what was happening historically at the time – the effect of industrialism on the people. Lawrence's description shows that when people replace nature with industry, they loose their integrity and wholeness.

consider when the text was written

Setting and environment

The setting and environment are essential in establishing the theme of this passage. This is a 'dismal' scene in which the miners' living conditions are described with emotive and negative adjectives: 'squalid', 'dismal', 'appalling', 'awful', 'stark'. It is even an effort for the car to approach such an area as it 'ploughed uphill'. Lawrence uses a simile to reinforce the depressing scene 'as if dismalness had soaked through and through everything' and the inclusion of words like 'death', horror', 'iron railings' and 'prison' help to establish the dreadful claustrophobic nature of this mining town.

use the text for evidence

Perhaps the most powerful tool Lawrence uses to reveal the dismal town is his use of colour. The passage is dominated by the colour black, just as the coal dominates the town. The town is immediately established as dirty and polluted with its 'exhaust vapour in the air' and 'smoke on the rain', but the depressing blackness of the town is stressed by the repetition of the colour throughout the passage: 'blackened brick dwellings, the black slate roofs … the mud black with coal-dust, the pavements wet and black', 'blackened brick' and 'blackened shrubs'.

The only other colours mentioned are the green at the beginning of the passage, which is quickly suppressed by the word 'dismal' and the 'greenish and raspberry glass' of the chapel and the 'expensive pink brick' of the school. These colours are not strong or bright and do not bring substance to the scene – the green is only 'ish' and the raspberry and pink are pallid and pale.

The other senses around Connie are also miserable. The sound of the 'strange bawling yell' and 'queer mechanical yells' of the children singing emphasises the lack of intuition and sensitivity among the mining community, even in the young. Connie feeling 'rather chilly' reinforces this dark, depressing, dirty soulless scene.

a personal response is important

Narratorial voice

The narrator is third person, and is omniscient. We learn that Connie has her 'heart in her boots', and much of the commentary is seen through Connie's eyes. The narrator enters into Connie's mind as the comments about the people in the mining town seem to come directly from Connie herself and the description is very much her interpretation of her surroundings rather than an objective, impartial view.

Characterisation

The scene focuses briefly on Connie. She is deeply affected by her surroundings, finding them squalid and depressing. The children's singing particularly affects her.

Language style

The passage is characterised by repetition and listing. These are used to convey the dominance of the blackened features of the town: 'the blackened brick dwellings, the black slate roofs glistening their sharp edges, the mud black with coal-dust, the pavements wet and black'. Repetition is also used to emphasise the town's hideousness 'ugly, ugly, ugly' and to stress its 'dismal' nature with 'through and through' lending weight to the description. Grammatical parallelism is also used to stress the miners' deprivation: 'The utter negation of natural beauty, the utter negation of the gladness of life, the utter absence of the instinct for shapely beauty ... the utter death of the human intuitive faculty' and 'It was not like savages ... it was not like animals ... It was like nothing on earth'.

questions often focus on use of language

45 minutes

Use your knowledge

1 Identify which part of the twentieth century your novel belongs to and list all the characteristics and literary features of that period which it includes.

2 What were the key historical happenings of the time and what influence do you feel they had on the novel?

3 Examine the hero or heroine. How are his/her thoughts and feelings described and presented in the text? Are they conveyed successfully? Do you empathise with them?

4 How is time handled? Does the beginning of the story occur at the beginning of the novel?

5 What is the theme of the novel? Is this consistent with the common themes of the era?

6 Do you feel that the novel could be read and understood by any reader, or are there some allusions that only a certain audience might understand?

7 How is the novel innovative in its form or use of language? Do features that are usually considered 'bad English', such as repetition of words, occur?

8 Is a moral message being made? If so, what kind of moral message do you feel this is?

Poetry Toolbox

20 minutes

Test your knowledge

1 Thinking of the subject matter of poetry, rather than poetic form, in your experience of reading poetry, name two different types of poem.

2 What name is given to the narrator of a poem?

3 Similes and metaphors are both examples of _____ .

4 Provide the correct literary term for the following definitions:
The repetition of consonant sounds in a poem is called _____ .
The repetition of vowel sounds in a poem is called _____ .

5 The meaning in lines of poetry sometimes ends with the line and sometimes extends to the next line. What two literary terms can you use to describe this?

6 What is metre?

7 What is the difference between masculine and feminine rhyme?

Answers

1 any two of the following: story-telling, argumentative, observation, emotion 2 the persona 3 imagery 4 alliteration, assonance 5 end-stopped and run-on 6 the rhythm in a line of poetry created by stressed and unstressed syllables 7 Masculine rhyming words have one syllable and feminine rhymes have several.

✔ **If you got them all right, skip to page 59**

30 minutes

Improve your knowledge

In the Poetry Toolbox chapter in *AS English in a Week*, we looked at the literary tools used by poets in creating poetry. The key difference you will need to demonstrate at A2 level is that you are able to evaluate as well as show awareness of the literary devices used. It is not sufficient to identify a simile, you must show how the simile contributes to the poem.

Key points from AS in a Week
Poetry
                pages 54–58

always ask yourself why a feature is effective

1 There are various different types of poems:

- poems that tell a story

- poems based on arguments

- poems based on observations

- poems based on emotions.

A first step to understanding poetry is to identify which type of poem you are studying and then to ask yourself what you feel the poem is about. Once you have an idea of this, you should ask yourself what is interesting about the words used and why you feel the poet has used them. You should concentrate on the words that you find striking or that are repeated or that contrast. If you cannot understand why you have found a word striking, try substituting a similar word to see how it affects the meaning of the poem. You can also look closely at the everyday usage of the word and how that meaning may have been exploited in the context of the poem.

2 A persona is a specially made voice that speaks in a poem, usually indicated by the presence of an 'I' in the poem. The persona need not be the poet (just as a first person narrator in a novel is not the author) and there can be more than one persona. You will need to identify the persona(s) and examine their attitude to the subject matter of the poem. You can use the term tone to describe the persona's mood, voice, manner, attitude and outlook.

3 In *AS English in a Week*, you learnt how to recognise imagery in the form of similes and metaphors. At A2 level you need to be able to show how images are used to create particular effects and how they contribute to the atmosphere and meaning of the poem as a whole. Similarly, when inanimate things are given human qualities, known as personification, you should try to describe how the poet has shown that the world is alive with feeling and emotion. A good phrase to use to describe this is pathetic fallacy (when human feelings are given to objects).

4 As well as looking closely at the meaning of words, in poetry you should pay close attention to their sounds, since sometimes the sound of a word is linked to its meaning. It is therefore important to spot alliteration (the repetition of consonant sounds), assonance (the repetition of vowel sounds) and onomatopoeia (when the word itself makes the sound that it refers to). The sounds often help to reflect what is going on in a poem at the time.

the sound of words is important to the meaning of the poem

5 You will notice that lines of poetry differ in that in some the meaning runs on to the next line and in some it does not. You need to concentrate on what effect this has on the meaning of the poem. End-stopped lines usually sound firm and finished because meanings are complete within them. Run-on lines create a feeling of expectation because at the close of the line, the meaning is not complete. Usually, this reflects the feeling conveyed by the content of the poem.

6 In a line of poetry, there is a sequence of stressed and unstressed syllables. Put together, these create a rhythm and the rhythm is called metre. The various different types of poetic rhythm can be found in the Poetry Toolbox chapter in *AS English in a Week*. You should concentrate on how the metre contributes to the poem as a whole, especially if the metre varies in a particular part of the poem. Metre and rhythm can have an effect on the meaning of the poem because they convey the 'voice'.

The rhyme scheme in a poem can set a pattern and some of these patterns have been given names – you will find these on page 55 of *AS English in a Week*. However, at A2 level, you must not only be able to recognise the rhyme scheme, you must comment on its influence on the atmosphere of the poem.

There are fundamentally two types of rhyme. Masculine rhymes have one syllable (cat/fat) and feminine rhymes have more than one syllable (moaning/groaning). Masculine rhyme often sounds complete and definite, whilst feminine rhyme sounds lyrical and musical. The ear wants to hear the completeness of two words rhyming – the rhyme can connect words together and emphasise their existence. Half-rhyme provides a discord, in that the words nearly rhyme, but don't quite. It therefore often reflects a sense of unease that is present in the mood of the poem.

the ear likes to hear the harmony of rhyme

Poetry Toolbox

60 minutes

Use your knowledge

Look closely at the poems that you are studying and answer the following questions.

1 Identify which type of poem each is and underline all the words that you find interesting or which caught your attention. Make brief notes on why you think these words are striking, using any literary terminology that you think is appropriate.

2 Identify whether each poem has a persona, and if so, how this affects the mood of the poem. How would you describe the tone of each poem?

3 Identify any imagery, symbolism and personification and carefully consider why the poet has used these literary features. What overall effect do they have on each poem?

4 How do sounds contribute to the meaning of the poems?

5 What are the effects of end-stopped and run-on lines?

6 What kinds of rhythms are used and how do they reflect the emotions of the poems?

7 Write about any rhymes you think are particularly successful and about how the form of the stanzas is appropriate to the meaning of the poem.

60 minutes

Test your knowledge

Read the following poem carefully. How does Owen portray the plight of the soldiers effectively?

Anthem for Doomed Youth

What passing-bells for those who die as cattle?
Only the monstrous anger of the guns.
Only the stuttering rifles' rapid rattle
Can patter out their hasty orisons.
No mockeries now for them: no prayers or bells,
Nor any voice of mourning save the choirs –
The shrill, demented choirs of wailing shells;
And bugles calling for them from sad shires.

What candles may be held to speed them all?
Not in the hands of boys, but in their eyes
Shall shine the holy glimmers of good-byes.
The pallor of girls' brows shall be their pall;
Their flowers the tenderness of patient minds
And each slow dusk a drawing-down of blinds.

Wilfred Owen

Answers

See Poetry Application Improve your Knowledge pages 61–63 for answers.

If you got them all right, skip to page 64

Improve your knowledge

You should always analyse the words in the title carefully. An anthem is a national song, one which brings a group of people together and gives them an identity. This poem is therefore a song which unites the soldiers. The word 'youth' suggests the soldiers have a hopeful and fulfilling future, yet the word 'doomed' contradicts this and introduces contrast – the soldiers, though young, are not 'youthful'. Their futures are marred with the constant threat of death which is all around them. The poem seems to highlight the barbaric circumstances of war, here emphasised by a comparison of the treatment of the dead soldiers on the battlefield and the Christian practices of burying the dead.

Key points from AS in a Week
Poetry Application
                pages 59–63

There is an extended metaphor running through this poem. The ugly burial of the dead soldiers is compared with the traditional ceremony at a Christian funeral. The poet selects various aspects of the service and finds a (usually disturbing) parallel on the battlefield. Words which indicate the metaphor are 'passing bells', 'prayers', 'bells', 'voice of mourning', 'bugles' and 'candles'. Every aspect of the funeral is therefore present, but the sound of shells replaces the choir of boys singing hymns, the only candle light is found in the soldier's eyes and the flowers and wreaths are represented by the patience and tenderness of others.

A simile is used in the first line. The poet compares the death of the soldiers to that of slaughtered cattle. This suggests that the soldiers are killed in great numbers and that their bodies are treated like carcasses rather than with the respect that human bodies deserve.

The last line introduces a new metaphor. The image of the drawn blinds has several implications. Obviously, for many soldiers, the blinds are drawn because they have lost their lives. Drawing the curtains or blinds traditionally is a sign of a death in a household and therefore this phrase also represents the mourning of the living soldiers for those who have died. Living soldiers may also feel a 'drawing-down' of their own emotions – they have watched fellow soldiers die appalling, painful deaths and therefore they need to separate themselves from such horror simply to keep their sanity. The blinds close out the horrors of war.

make sure that you mention the contribution to the poem as a whole of the various techniques used

The vocabulary used in the first stanza collocates (brings together) strongly, in that the words are negative and relate to the disturbance of the mind – 'monstrous', 'mourning', 'demented', 'wailing'. In the second stanza, the vocabulary again collocates strongly – 'tenderness, 'patient' – creating a different effect and atmosphere to the first stanza. It is as if the disturbing emotional state of the first stanza is resolved in the second.

The connotations of the words used create sharp contrasts between a usual type of burial ceremony and the reality of death in war. The peaceful, religious, almost romantic connotations that we hold with choirs, bells, candles and flowers emphasise the harshness of the 'wailing shells' and the sounds of gunfire. The connotations of the choir boys' innocence and purity is extended to the soldiers – they are no more than boys themselves.

A striking use of sound can be found in line three. The alliteration of 'r' and repetition of hard consonant sounds ('t' and 'p') of the 'stuttering rifles' rapid rattle' mirrors the sound of the repeated gun fire, creating onomatopoeia as the reader can hear the sound of the guns in the poem through the sound of the words used to describe it.

The guns are personified and given the human emotion of anger. This establishes the idea that, in angrily firing themselves, the guns are to blame for the deaths, rather than the soldiers. We are allowed to feel our compassion for the soldiers, forgetting that each one has probably killed another to save his own life.

your own opinion is important – but make sure you support it with evidence from the poem

Each stanza starts with a question which is then answered by the poet himself. The questions prompt the reader to consider carefully how the soldiers are treated in death and to judge their treatment against the norms of our society. To emphasise the tragedy of his answer, the poet uses repetition of negative words ('nor' and 'no') and words that emphasise limitation ('only').

The first stanza contains eight lines, the second stanza contains six and the first questioning line of each stanza is longer than the others. This is intricately linked with the rhyme scheme. The rhythm of the poem is agitated and inconsistent. This reflects the disturbing nature of the subject matter of the poem, not allowing the reader to feel at ease with the music of the language. The rhyme scheme of the poem is similarly unsettling. The first stanza consists of two sets of quatrains (ababcdcd) whilst the first four lines of the second stanza almost reflect the style of a sonnet (abba) with two rhyming couplets to complete the poem. The unease is also emphasised by the half-rhymes in the poem ('shell'/'shires').

Use your knowledge

Read the extract opposite from Christina Rosetti's 'Goblin Market', a narrative poem about two sisters, one of whom (Laura) buys and eats the forbidden, cursed fruit from the Goblin Men. Annotate the poem with reference to:

- metaphors

- similes

- symbols

- alliteration

- repetition of words

- rhyme scheme.

I ate and ate my fill,
Yet my mouth waters still;
To-morrow night I will buy more; and kissed her
'Have done with sorrow;
I'll bring you plums tomorrow
Fresh on their mother twigs,
Cherries worth getting;
You cannot think what fits
My teeth have met in,
What melons ice-cold
Piled on a dish of gold
Too huge for me to hold,
What peaches with a velvet nap,
Pellucid grapes without one seed:
Odorous indeed must be the mead
Whereon they grow, and pure the wave they drink
With lilies at the brink,
And sugar-sweet their sap.'
*   Golden head by golden head,*
Like two pigeons in one nest
Folded in each other's wings,
They lay down in their curtained bed:
Like two blossoms on one stem
Like two flakes of new-fall'n snow,
Like two wands of ivory
Tipped with gold for awful kings.
Moon and stars gazed in at them,
Wind sang to them lullaby,
Lumbering owls forbore to fly,
Not a bat flapped to and fro
Round their nest:
Cheek to cheek and breast to breast
Locked together in one nest.

20 minutes

Test your knowledge

1 Chaucer was writing in the _____ century.

2 Chaucer wrote *The Canterbury Tales,* which are a collection of

_____

_____.

3 The narrative voice who occasionally intervenes is the _____. He is important because _____

_____.

4 Five characters from The Canterbury Tales are:

_____   _____

_____   _____

_____.

5 In my study of Chaucer I should note how the character's _____ relates to the _____ they tell.

6 *The Canterbury Tales* consists mainly of _____ pentameter lines and _____ couplets.

7 I should always use quotations from an edition which uses _____ English rather than modern English.

8 I need to show the examiners my understanding of _____ devices employed, _____ delineation and Chaucer's narrative skills.

Answers

1 fourteenth **2** prologues and tales told by various characters from differing social classes to win a competition for the best tale set by their host, Chaucer **3** host, he provides the framework for the tales, adding realism and purpose for the narratives that follow **4** For a full list of characters see pages 67–68. **5** prologue, tale **6** iambic, heroic **7** Middle **8** poetic, character

✔ **If you got them all right, skip to page 73**

Chaucer Toolbox and Application

60 minutes

Improve your knowledge

1 Chaucer was born between 1340 and 1345 and died in 1400. During this period major events such as The Hundred Years War, The Black Death, The Peasant's Revolt and the deposition of Richard II occurred. Chaucer was writing in a time of great change, not only historically but also in terms of the progress of the English language. French was the language of the court and English was seen as common. Chaucer's decision to write in his vernacular, English (we call it Middle English) was revolutionary. He was taught in French and most literature would have been either in Latin or French. Chaucer was so popular in his time and contributed so much to English literature that John Dryden called him the 'father of English poetry'. Chaucer was interested in all forms of living and experienced life to the full. The diverse range of characters and situations he represents in *The Canterbury Tales* shows his interest in:

- the relationship between the natural world and the human world

- how life was organised in terms of hierarchies

- the workings and effects of the social class system.

2 *The Canterbury Tales* is much shorter than Chaucer originally intended it to be when he started it in 1387. We cannot be certain of the correct order of the tales. The situation as described in the General Prologue is that a band of travellers to Canterbury meet in a public house in London. The host invites them all to tell a tale and offers a prize for the best tale. The band of travellers includes:

Genteel class:	Knight and son
	Squire and attendant yeomen
Church representatives:	Prioress
	Nun
	personal Chaplain
	Monk
	Friar
Others:	Merchant

Oxford Clerk

Sergeant of the Law

Franklin

Guildsman

Tradesman

Widow (Wife of Bath)

Parson

Reeve

Miller

Summoner

Pardoner

You are not expected to know all of these characters, but you should be aware that Chaucer is able to write from a multiplicity of viewpoints successfully and skilfully.

3 Narrative voice

The overall persona is the host who describes himself in the General Prologue as a portly, bookish, well meaning, dim-witted man, who may not entertain his audience to their satisfaction. Notice how the host undermines his own ability; the effect is that when we hear the tales we are pleased because they are better than expected. By using a persona like the host to convey the tales to the audience, Chaucer the poet distances himself from the opinions expressed by the various characters and cannot therefore be blamed for any unconventional or unpopular views.

Look for the following distinctive features in the narrative voice telling the tale:

- tone: satirical, plaintive, accusatory, humorous
- rhythm: heroic couplets to represent units of meaning
- imagery: use of commercial, religious, sexual images
- mood: sorrowful, regretful, anxious, judgmental
- structure: monologues, interruptions.

Chaucer Toolbox and Application

One key thing to remember is that even though you may be studying 'The Miller's Tale', for example, it is Chaucer who controls the narrative. There will be conflicts between speakers and their ideas; again remember Chaucer is the puppet master and it is he who manipulates your point of view, although the opinions the characters express are not necessarily his own.

 Characters are numerous and diverse. Chaucer manipulates our views of the characters by exaggerating one particular characteristic or aspect to their personality. This means that the characterisation is almost a caricature. Look at this extract – a description of the Wife of Bath from the General Prologue:

> For she was gap-toothed, if you take my meaning.
>
> Comfortably on an ambling horse she sat,
>
> Well-wimpled, wearing on her head a hat
>
> That might have been a shield in size and shape
>
> A riding-skirt round her enormous hips,
>
> Also a pair of sharp spurs on her feet.
>
> In company, how she could laugh and joke!
>
> No doubt she knew all the cures for love,
>
> For at that game she was a past mistress.

Chaucer's audience would have thought this indicated a high sex drive

Notice the exaggerated trait here is the vastness of the wife, physically and in terms of personality and sexuality.

5 Relationship between character and tale

Avoid considering the character's prologue as distinct from the tale they tell. Try to keep in mind the purpose of the narrators of *The Canterbury Tales*, to win a competition for telling the best story. Consider how the tale a character tells is appropriate to the different aspects of their character.

Chaucer Toolbox and Application

 6 **Style**

When you are writing about Chaucer's style, keep firmly in mind that you are analysing the language – everything you have revised in the Poetry Toolbox chapter is very relevant. The following features are particularly applicable to Chaucer:

remember The Canterbury Tales was intended to be read aloud to a live audience!

- intimate conversational undertone

> *But yet I praye to all this* **compaignye**   (company)
>
> *If that I speke after my fantyse*
>
> *For mine* **entente** *nis but for to* **pleye**.   (intent, play)
>
> *Now, sire, now wol I tell you forth my tale.*

- rhetorical questions:

> *Wher can ye seye, in any manere age,*
>
> *That heighe God* **defended** *mariage*   (condemned)
>
> *By expres word? I pray you, telleth me.*
>
> *Or where he comanded virgintee?*

- description:

> *Her* **coverchiefs** *ful fine weren of ground-*   (head scarf)
>
> *I dorste swere they* **weyeden** *ten pound-*   (weighed)
>
> *That on a Sunday weren upon her head.*
>
> *Her* **hosen** *weren of fin scarlet red,*   (hosiery)
>
> *Ful* **streite yteyd**, *and shoes ful moiste and newe.* (tightly laced)
>
> *Boold was her face, and fair, and reed of* **hewe**. (hue)

The rhythm in *The Canterbury Tales* is iambic pentameter. Chaucer was the first poet to use the way the French wrote poetry (French versification) within the boundaries of his language, what we now call Middle English. Chaucer was the first poet to use the rhyming pentameter also known as the heroic couplet. This is the principle meter for *The Canterbury Tales*.

look this up in AS in a Week Poetry Toolbox if you don't remember!

Chaucer Toolbox and Application

7 Middle English is so called because it comes between Old English (*Bewoulf*, for example) and modern English. You should try reading Chaucer's poetry aloud because it is only then you develop a sense of his rhythmical skill and note how effective it is as a storytelling medium. Chaucer's poetry was always meant to be heard rather than read, as printing presses did not exist. To help with your reading remember the following points about Middle English:

- Sounds are often similar to modern English.

- Unfamiliar words and references are usually explained in footnotes.

- Some words may be familiar but the meanings will have changed (e.g. 'defended' in Middle English means 'condemned' but in modern English means 'protected').

- The syntax (order of words) may not be familiar – try to establish why Chaucer has ordered the words in that way.

- Listen to a tape recording either from your school, local library or book shop.

Words that occur frequently are well worth remembering:

er	before
hir	their
eek/eke	and also
siker	sure

When reading aloud, try to remember how personal pronouns are pronounced, this will help you to appreciate the rhythm of the lines.

he	*hay*
she	*shay*
me	*may*
they	*thy-ee*
I	*ee*
my	*mee*
mine	*meen*

look at the back of your Chaucer text – you may discover a glossary, if so use it!

Chaucer Toolbox and Application

 8 Frequent questions regarding Chaucer's *The Canterbury Tales* are:

How does the Wife of Bath maintain the interest of the audience?

- discussion of conventional material in an unconventional way

- humour and wit

- sharply drawn characterisations of her husbands.

OR

How appropriate to her character is the tale the Wife of Bath has been given to narrate by Chaucer?

The Wife of Bath's prologue reveals the following aspects of her character that are also concerns in the tale:

- Subject of marriage.

- The Wife of Bath's main contention is regarding the authority of male over female in sex, legal issues and marriage.

- Search for a suitable marriage partner.

- Romantic conclusion to the tale mirrors the wish-fulfilment of the Wife of Bath's marriage to a younger man in her prologue.

Always remember the following:

- Chaucer's narrative skill – the stories are amusing and entertaining; consider how appropriate the story is to the teller as in the example above.

- Narrative voice – Chaucer uses personas as a device to convey the prologues and the tales, but remember that it is Chaucer who is the puppeteer.

- Character delineation – one aspect of the character is usually exaggerated; this is effective because it allows the audience to appreciate their personality in a relatively short amount of text.

- Poetic devices – analyse the text closely for features of speech, imagery, metaphors and similes.

read the character descriptions in the General Prologue

remember TRIMS!

Chaucer Toolbox and Application

45 minutes

Use your knowledge

1 Chaucer was interested in _____ and this is demonstrated through _____ and plot.

2 What theme does the prologue and tale you are studying explore?

3 What are the distinctive stylistic features of the speaker in the prologue and tale you are studying?

4 Describe five features of the character you are studying.

5 How is the character's prologue an appropriate match to the their tale?

6 What does the use of the heroic couplet in the tale you are studying convey?

7 In order to fully appreciate the rhythms and metre of the prologue and tale I must attempt to _____ .

8 I must consider the following points in response to an essay title such as:

'The Wife of Bath's prologue is twice as long as her tale. Why do you think Chaucer gives more emphasis to her prologue than to the story she tells?'

(a) The achievements of the _____ .

(b) The way the _____ mirrors the prologue.

(c) The effectiveness of Chaucer's character _____ .

120 minutes

The following extract is from the opening chapter of Daphne Du Maurier's *Rebecca*. Identify the key literary devices used in this passage and comment on their effectiveness in creating atmosphere.

Last night I dreamt I went to Manderley again. It seemed to me I stood by the iron gate leading to the drive, and for a while I could not enter, for the way was barred to me. There was a padlock and a chain upon the gate. I called in my dream to the lodge-keeper, and had no answer, and peering closer through the rusted spokes of the gate I saw that the lodge was uninhabited.

No smoke came from the chimney, and the little lattice windows gaped forlorn. Then, like all dreamers, I was possessed of a sudden with supernatural powers and passed like a spirit through the barrier before me. The drive wound away in front of me, twisting and turning as it had always done, but as I advanced I was aware that a change had come upon it; it was narrow and unkept, not the drive that we had known. At first, I was puzzled and did not understand, and it was only when I bent my head to avoid the low swinging branch of a tree that I realized what had happened. Nature had come into her own again and, little by little, in her stealthy, insidious way had encroached upon the drive with long, tenacious fingers. The woods, always a menace even in the past, had triumphed in the end. They crowded, dark and uncontrolled, to the borders of the drive. The beeches with white, naked limbs leant close to one another, their branches intermingled in a strange embrace, making a vault above my head like the archway of a church. And there were other trees as well, trees that I did not recognize, squat oaks and tortured elms that straggled cheek by jowl with the beeches, and had thrust themselves out of the quiet earth, along with monster shrubs and plants, none of which I remembered.

The drive was a ribbon now, a thread of its former self, with gravel surface gone, and choked with grass and moss. The trees had thrown out long branches, making an impediment to progress; the gnarled roots looked like skeleton claws. Scattered here and again amongst this jungle growth I would recognize shrubs that had been landmarks in our time, things of culture and grace, hydrangeas whose blue heads had been famous. No hand had checked their progress, and they had gone native now, rearing to monster height without a bloom, black and ugly as the nameless parasites that grew beside them.

Pointers

You should have noted the following important points:

- The passage concerns the account of a dream in which a house is revisited. The dream is disturbing in that the house is now unoccupied and derelict and nature has taken over in a menacing and frightening way.

- The scene is set immediately by identifying that the account that follows is a dream – we are allowed a first-hand account of the dream through the first person narrator.

- The introduction of the name 'Manderley' creates suspense in the reader as we do not know what this place is and how it is of significance to the narrator.

- There are many literary techniques used to portray the lack of human presence in the scene and the intimidating way nature has taken over. Here are some of them, with an evaluation of their effects on the passage:

Technique	Example	Evaluation
Personification	'windows gaped forlorn'	The windows are given human emotions to show that even inanimate objects are sad and pitiful because the house has fallen to dereliction.
	'long, tenacious fingers'	By describing nature as human, the writer shows nature's power but also allows nature to be something menacing and intimidating.
	'The beeches with white, naked limbs leant closely to one another.'	These trees seem to be silver beeches, represented by the 'white', but to the dreamer, their branches are like arms and legs and they have the ability to conspire together like pack animals. Again this shows the power and force of nature when it is allowed to take over.
	'had thrust themselves out of the quiet earth'	Here, not only are the trees given human characteristics, but a contrast is set up between the trees' aggressive movement and the peaceful 'quiet' earth from which they are born.
	'choked with grass and moss'	Nature is given the power to murder – a powerful piece of personification.

Simile	'like a spirit'	As if the narrator is ghost-like. There is a strong suggestion of death.
	'like the archway of a church'	Creates a good visual impression, but also suggests the dark, mystery and death of a church atmosphere.
	'the gnarled roots looked like skeleton claws'	This is a clear association with death and shows that the dreamer interprets the scene in a macabre and deathly way.
Metaphor	'their branches intermingled in a strange embrace, making a vault above my head'	The symbolism here is contrasting and quite macabre. The trees are described as if they are embracing, but in doing so, they create a picture of death – a vault.
	'the drive as a ribbon now, a thread of its former self'	The image of a ribbon is used to show the diminution of the drive due to nature encroaching on its space. The drive represents human control over nature – laying a path to make an easy track through nature to the house. But nature has taken over this track and the image is continued by emphasising its reduced size from a ribbon to a 'thread'.
Emotive words	'Stealthy, insidious' 'encroached' 'a menace' 'they crowded, dark and uncontrolled' 'squat oaks and tortured elms' 'monster shrubs and plants' 'monster height without a bloom' 'black and ugly'	All of these words indicate the menacing, intimidating way Nature has taken over the scene and the extent to which Nature now dominates. The scene is dark and 'ugly', which helps to pursue the idea of death, and the plants and trees have certainly become frightening and disturbing to the mind of the dreamer.
	'things of culture and grace'	This provides a contrast by describing the plants when they were controlled by humans in a positive way.

Exam Practice Questions

60 minutes

per section

Post-1900 prose

Looking carefully at your novel, how do you feel it is innovative in its form, language and content?

Poetry

Examine in detail one theme which runs through six or seven of the poems that you have studied and explain how this theme is handled differently.

Pre-1900 Prose Novel

1 Select an extract from your novel that effectively demonstrates the social, historical or cultural concerns.

2 Select an extract from your novel that demonstrates the literary style of the author.

Drama

1 Look closely at the first scene of your play. Discuss the dramatic techniques the playwright uses to present the exposition of the play.

2 A critic has said that 'the function of drama is to educate and entertain.' Discuss to what extent this can be found true of the drama text you are studying.

Chaucer

1 Do you consider Chaucer to be 'a master storyteller who sharply delineates characters, often for comic effect'? Discuss this view with reference to the prologue and tale that you are studying.

2 Would you agree that the most important aspect of Chaucer's writing is the delivery of a moral message? Discuss this view with reference to the prologue and tale that you are studying.

Use your Knowledge Answers

Essay Writing

1 (a) quotation
(b) direct
(c) passage-based
(d) treatment

2 (b)

3 The poet describes the scene of a bomb attack by using imagery of punctuation to represent the chaos of the scene and of the poet's mind. The physical look of the punctuation marks present the visual side of the scene and their meaning and use in a sentence represents the state of the poet's mind. When the bomb explodes, the 'nuts, bolts, nails' look like exclamation marks to the poet as they fly through the air; the meaning of an exclamation mark also represents the poet's surprise and shock. The centre of the explosion itself looks like an asterisk, with its solid burning centre and flames reaching out. An asterisk also marks an important part of a text, reflecting the significance of the bomb in this scene. The machine gun fire is likened to a 'hyphenated line' and the poet provides a visual representation of the sound with the dots at the end of the third line. Full stops and colons provide a long pause in a sentence and therefore it is apt that the poet uses these two forms of punctuation to describe how the streets are blocked and he cannot escape the scene. The punctuation that flies all around him in chaos is mirrored by the chaos within his mind – the poet is shocked and cannot even form a sentence in his own head. Water imagery is used to describe the movement of the flying debris, as in 'it was raining' punctuation and there is 'a fount of broken type'.

4 any four of the following: stage directions, props, costumes, lighting, soliloquy

5 'dominant' = overriding, prevailing, main, key
'influence' = control, power
'plot' = main storyline, action
'subplot' = secondary storyline
'hearsay' = rumour, report, unfounded information
'far' = much
'agree' = have the same opinion, share the view

6 Rumour certainly has an overriding power over the main and secondary story lines in *Much Ado About Nothing*.

7 (b)

8 Any four of the following: concise, succinct, summary, main points, key points, argument, draw together, answer the question.

Style Toolbox

Change the tense throughout the essay from past to present.

Swap colloquial phrases such as 'showing up' and 'be around' for more formal words and phrases such as 'emphasising' and 'be in attendance'.

Change the first person 'I' to the third person in the commentary. For example, lines 3 to 4 could read 'Perhaps this shows that Gatsby is truly "great", as the title would suggest.'

The narrator in a novel is not the author as the student has assumed in line 5.

Change all the abbreviated words, such as 'they're' and 'he's' to their full two-word versions.

Change the phrase 'a lot' to 'a great deal'.

Don't just list literary devices – explain how they affect the text.

Make sure you spell correctly – 'similes' and 'F Scott Fitzgerald'.

Drama Toolbox

The answers you have given are specific to your text. If you have struggled with any of the questions on structure, go back to the drama chapters in *AS English in a Week* to help you work through them. Be honest and ensure that you have the structure of the plot firmly in your mind before you begin to work on the Drama Application and the Drama Examination Question Toolbox chapters.

Use your Knowledge Answers

Drama Application

1 Review your essay plans. Check the following features:

- every comment should be relevant to the question

- check that you have used textual evidence to support your comments

- check that you have analysed the use of the textual evidence.

2 Compare your answers with the example paragraphs in the Improve your knowledge section. Again, ensure that your paragraph contains a key comment, supporting textual evidence and analysis of the textual evidence.

3 Thinking critically will help you to prepare for the questions you will get in the examination. Check your answers with a revision partner, a teacher or even a parent. Have you formulated an appropriate statement and are you able to use the text to support or argue against it?

4 A critical edition of your drama text will often provide you with key information about the context of the play you are studying. Make sure that you have read the information and are able to write about it in your own words.

Drama Examination Question Toolbox

1 A genre-based question will ask me to consider how the play I am studying fits into the genre. I will need to understand the generic features and discuss how the dramatist has used those features in the play I am studying.

2 A thematic-based question will ask me to look at how the theme is presented, developed and resolved throughout the play. I will need to look at the organisation of the plot, the characters' involvement in the theme and the language associated with the theme.

3 A character-based question will ask me look at how the character is constructed, to consider the character's actions, interactions, and motivations in the drama. I will also need to analyse carefully the character's use of language and their contribution to the plot of the play.

4 A statement-based question will provide me with an opinion of the play I am studying. I will need to evaluate that statement to see how far I think it applies to the play and also offer my own judgement.

5 A close scene analysis question will either provide me with an extract(s) or ask me to choose an extract(s) from the play I am studying and require me to state how far I agree with the statement that has been given. I should also consider how the extract fits into the play as a whole.

6 An audience-based question will ask me to consider the responses of the audience and to discuss the methods the dramatist uses to manipulate the audience's responses.

Prose Toolbox

The answers to these questions will vary from one novel to the next. If you have experienced difficulties in answering the questions, you should re-read the Use your knowledge answers section in *AS English In a Week* and consider the following points:

- Remember that you must read all of the novel for you to be able to think about it cohesively.

- Try not to take a long time to read the novel as you will find it difficult to track the development of the plot and the characters.

- As you read, continuously ask yourself why characters behave in certain ways and why events are organised as they are.

- Try to see the novel as a whole and not as a series of isolated incidences.

- Consider how you feel about characters and events as you read.

- Make a note of aspects of the novel that you find interesting (including quotes) on your first reading – this will help you hold your concentration and help you to link ideas throughout the novel.

Pre-1900 Prose Application

1 Remind yourself of the literary features from the Prose Toolbox. How many did you manage to remember? A useful revision tip is to build a library of index cards for each literary feature, find evidence from the text and write a few key phrases on the effect of the literary feature. This will also help you to remember key quotations for closed text examinations.

2 Refer back to the Improve your knowledge section, number 2, for the table of types of novels. You may find that your novel is a mixture of types. If this is the case, ensure that you have supporting evidence to prove it.

3 Look again at the exemplar paragraphs in the Improve your knowledge section and compare your answers. Ensure that you have incorporated a key point, a textual reference and an evaluation of the textual reference.

4 Making up questions is an excellent way to place yourself in the seat of the examiner. Examiners are not looking to catch you out or trip you up. The questions they provide merely require a sound understanding of the text you are studying and the confidence to offer your own informed opinion. They are looking to reward your learning and the long hours of revision and will be encouraged by the awarding body to be positive in their marking.

5 Many students ignore the importance of context. Make sure that you do your research on the text and that any points you have made are relevant to the question. Avoid quoting historical events that are really nothing to do with the text you are studying. Be prepared, do that extra reading and you will be rewarded in the exam. Look at the paragraph in the Improve your knowledge section, number 5, to help you gain an insight into how you can incorporate context in an essay.

Post-1900 Prose Application

Every novel is unique and because of the enormous range of styles and acceptance of innovative form in the twentieth century, the answers to these questions will be different for every novel.

Some students find analysing the modern novel difficult, especially as the fact that the novel was written recently means that there is little literary criticism to be read. This means that you must have confidence in your own ideas and use your own knowledge of what is and has been going on around you to make your own judgements.

Your relationship with the characters should be close – they are the mirror of society yesterday and today and therefore your affinity with them is important.

The themes of the novel may well relate to the concerns that you have in life, or depict the concerns of your parents or grandparents in past years.

The language will possibly reflect language use today – notice the acceptance of slang and dialectal forms and the rejection of 'standard' English as the only correct form of English.

The content may emphasise the progress made in embracing people of other cultures, religions, sexualities and classes.

The modern novel is what the reader wishes to make of it. Your interpretation is modern literary criticism!

Poetry Toolbox

The answers to these questions will obviously depend on the poetry that you are studying and every poem will provide different answers.

Some general hints that might help you are:

- Always try to write about the poem as a whole, rather than the sum of lots of bits.

- Find out when the poem was written and what styles of poetry writing were popular at the time.

- Bear in mind the historical era of the poem in interpreting its contents.

- You will find that older poems contain archaic language and words that you have not heard before. Be careful to find out how these words were pronounced so that you can make accurate comments about rhythm and rhyme.

Poetry Application

The poem has been annotated with comments you could have made.

I ate and ate my fill,   *a*

Yet my mouth waters still;   *a*

To-morrow night I will buy more; and kissed her   *c*

'Have done with sorrow;   *d*   irregular rhyme scheme reflecting content

I'll bring you plums tomorrow   *d*

Fresh on their mother twigs,   *e*

Cherries worth getting;   *f*

You cannot think what fits   *g*   metaphor showing unity

My teeth have met in,   *h*

What melons ice-cold   *i*

Piled on a dish of gold   *i*

Too huge for me to hold,   *i*

What peaches with a velvet nap,   *j*

Pellucid grapes without one seed: *k*   alliteration

Odorous indeed must be the mead   *k*

Whereon they grow, and pure the wave they drink   *l*

With lilies at the brink,   *l*

And sugar-sweet their sap.'   *j*

    Golden head by golden head,   *m*

Like two pigeons in one nest   *n*

Folded in each other's wings,   *o*

They lay down in their curtained bed: *m*

Like two blossoms on one stem   *p*

Like two flakes of new-fall'n snow,   *q*

Like two wands of ivory   *r*   natural similes

Tipped with gold for awful kings.   *o*

Moon and stars gazed in at them,   *p*

Wind sang to them lullaby,   *s*

Lumbering owls forbore to fly,   *s*

Not a bat flapped to and fro   *r*

Round their nest: *n*

Cheek to cheek and breast to breast   *n*

Locked together in one nest.   *n*

repetition

metaphor showing opulence

repetition of parallel images

Chaucer Toolbox and Application

Your answer will refer to the tale you are studying. Here we will use *The Wife of Bath's Tale* as an example.

1 human experience, character

2 marriage and the experience of women in Chaucer's society

3 wit, irony, parody, bawdiness

4 loquacity, honesty, brutality, argumentativeness

5 For the Wife of Bath, we could say that her main interest is authority over the male, reflected in the treatment of the knight by the ladies in the court and how he acquiesces to the old woman, finally offering her mastery.

6 succinct and focused units of meaning

7 listen to a recording, read the poetry aloud

8 (a) prologue
(b) tale
(c) delineation

Exam Practice Answers

Post-1900 Prose

To answer this question, you may find it helpful to consider where the beginning, middle and end of the novel are structured within the text and how the concept of time is handled. Closely examine the role of the narrator; is there any evidence of a stream of consciousness? The theme and content of the novel may be innovative in that they explore the modern world with a different perspective and this will probably be reflected in the language. Features such as repetition of words and slang which have been considered poor use of written English may be used in post-1900 novels to create a particular effect.

Poetry

Introduction

A useful first step is to identify the theme and to expand briefly on what the theme is about. You should then name the poems that you are going to write about, giving the examiner an idea of how you are going to structure your essay by identifying the poetic techniques that you will discuss in your narrative.

Middle section

Write a paragraph on each technique, making sure that you provide relevant quotes from the poems to support your ideas and ensuring that your points are relevant to answering the question. You should therefore make sure that your points are always targeted towards showing how the theme is either treated similarly or differently in the poems. It may be sensible to structure your answer so that you discuss all the elements that are similar in one section, and all the elements that are different in a second section.

Conclusion

Write a concise paragraph that provides a succinct answer to the question and summarise the middle section of your essay. You may include your own opinion if you wish.

Pre-1900 Prose

1 Ensure that you have completed the Pre-1900 Prose chapter beginning on page 41. The essay you have written should be focused on the cultural, social and historical concerns of your novel and therefore will be very specific. If you are struggling, divide an A3 sheet into three, label each section cultural, social and historical and produce your own definitions of the terms so you understand them. Go back through your novel and insert quotations that are appropriate for each of the sections. This will then give you an overview of how the novelist deals with each concern. From this, you can formulate an essay plan and then write your essay!

2 This question requires you to do a close critical reading on a section of text to see how well you appreciate the literary style of the author you are studying. You will find that the author is consistent in the use of language. For example, Hardy continually uses the external environment to mirror the emotions and situations of his characters. Ensure you have used the appropriate literary terms as explained in the Prose Toolbox, which begins on page 36.

Exam Practice Answers

Drama

1 This question asks you to focus on the first scene of the play and assess the effectiveness of the way in which the dramatist has established the main themes, characters, plot and setting of the play. You should ensure that you draw on all four of these aspects in your answer, again using appropriate terminology in your discussion. If you are struggling, remind yourself of the Drama Toolbox, Application and Examination Toolbox chapters beginning on page 13.

2 This statement-based question asks you to assess how far the play educates and entertains. You should ensure you tackle both aspects of the question and use appropriate textual extracts to support your view. Remember that you may consider the play to be more entertaining than educational and, as long as you have supported your view with evidence from the text, this is valid.

Chaucer

1 It is vital that you consider all parts of the question in your answer:

- Chaucer as a storyteller
- delineation of characters
- comic effect.

Your essay should cover all three aspects of the question with supporting textual evidence. Remember you can disagree with the idea of 'comic effect' if you consider that Chaucer is conveying a more serious message in the construction of characters. You must incorporate textual evidence and show the examiner how you have arrived at your point of view.

2 This question requires you to assess the purpose of the tale you are studying. You need to examine the tale and identify whether there is a moral message, what the moral message is and if you consider the moral message to be the most important feature of the tale or not.

Acknowledgements

Extract on page 74 reproduced with permission of Curtis Brown Ltd, London, on behalf of the Chichester Partnership. *Rebecca* © Daphne Du Maurier (1938) by Daphne Du Maurier.